"It takes eleven essays of lived
level, from the call of a new ch
ecosystem of a denomination, to bring a fuller picture of what it means to develop a posture *conducive* to receive sustaining grace from God and others. As you carefully read through these stories, you will find gems of engaging truth, reminding you God still opposes the proud but gives grace to the humble."

—JR WOODWARD
V3 Movement and author of *Creating a Missional Culture*

"Here's a book on sustainable ministry that is not a drab why-and-how-to-fundraise manual but instead a stirring invitation to imagine the precarity of new worshiping communities as a gift to the whole church. It will prove to be a fruitful conversation starter for all who are involved and invested in seeing new worshiping communities—and not-so-new worshiping communities—flourish.

—CHRISTOPHER B. JAMES
University of Dubuque Theological Seminary

"Hurray for Scott Hagley and his team for taking on the most challenging obstacle for most new worshiping communities, how to become sustainable for longer than the first couple of years. *Sustaining Grace* helps us to see that starting new churches is not an optional luxury item in the expense line for thriving churches. Instead it is essential for the sustainability of God's church in all its expressions."

—VERA KARN WHITE
1001 New Worshiping Communities
(Presbyterian Church [U.S.A.])

"This collection further invalidates the lie that church-starting is the activity of a singular leader. The 'mixed economy' of writers, writing from their various social locations, remind us of our inherent need for each other, from planter to judicatory leader, to join God in the mysterious work of ecclesial innovation."

—NICK WARNES
Cyclical INC and Cyclical LA

"*Sustaining Grace* offers a prophetic word in the midst of crisis and protest, when established churches are being forced to confront foundational questions about who we are as followers of Jesus Christ in this world. Early in the book, this possibility is offered: 'Perhaps the sudden vulnerability experienced by mainline and evangelical churches carries with it the prophetic and disruptive word of God.' If you're curious about seeing how the 'prophetic and disruptive word of God' may be at work in new worshiping communities and emerging congregations, this is the book for you!"

—CINDY KOHLMANN
223rd General Assembly, Presbyterian Church (U.S.A.)

Sustaining Grace

Sustaining Grace

Innovative Ecosystems
for New Faith Communities

Edited by
Scott J. Hagley
Karen Rohrer
and Michael Gehrling

Foreword by Nikki Collins

WIPF & STOCK • Eugene, Oregon

SUSTAINING GRACE
Innovative Ecosystems for New Faith Communities

Wipf & Stock
An Imprint of Wipf and Stock Publishers
199 W. 8th Ave., Suite 3
Eugene, OR 97401

www.wipfandstock.com

PAPERBACK ISBN: 978-1-5326-8759-4
HARDCOVER ISBN: 978-1-5326-8760-0
EBOOK ISBN: 978-1-5326-8761-7

Manufactured in the U.S.A. 06/22/20

Many of the church's most innovative leaders serve with great sacrifice. Some start new ministries and churches. Others provide creative, revitalizing leadership to legacy congregations. Some do this work for little or no pay. Others do it without the security of health insurance or retirement plans. Still others do it in contexts geographically far from family and close friends. To all of them, we dedicate this book.

Contents

Contributing Authors

In Order of Appearance

Scott J. Hagley
Associate Professor of Missiology at Pittsburgh Theological Seminary.

Karen Rohrer
Director of the Church Planting Initiative at Pittsburgh Theological Seminary, and previously Founding Co-pastor of Beacon Church in Philadelphia, PA.

Barry Ensign-George
Coordinator for Theology and Worship at the Presbyterian Mission Agency.

Michael Gehrling
Associate for 1001 New Worshiping Communities at the Presbyterian Mission Agency, and previously Founding Co-pastor of The Upper Room in Pittsburgh, PA.

Aisha Brooks-Lytle
Executive Presbyter at the Presbytery of Greater Atlanta, and previously Associate Pastor for Mission at Wayne Presbyterian Church and Organizing Pastor of The Common Place in Philadelphia, PA.

Kristine Stache
Associate Professor of Missional Leadership at Wartburg Seminary.

David Loleng	Director of Church Financial Literacy and Leadership at the Presbyterian Foundation.
Michael Moynagh	Consultant to the Church of England on the Greenhouse Initiative, and Associate Tutor at Wycliffe Hall, Oxford.
Beth Scibienski	Pastor at Grace Presbyterian Church in Kendall Park, NJ.
Jeya So	Founding Co-pastor at Anchor City Church in San Diego, CA.

Foreword

When I graduated from seminary, I did not imagine I would ever engage in the ministry of starting new churches. God had other ideas. After serving two beautiful and historic congregations in small towns, I became the wife of the organizing pastor of a parachute-style new church development. We were "dropped" into a context new to us to begin the work of forming spiritual community. After that, I worked with a team to launch a new worshipping community that also functioned as a coffee shop. Later, I served as the presbytery leader where a population boom had led to the start of half a dozen or so new congregations in the years before I arrived. Some are still thriving under second-generation leadership. Some had experienced internal crises and closed their doors or shifted their denominational alignment. A community of immigrants had been waiting to charter for years, and another young Anglo church was closed by the presbytery on the day I began my post. Although we did not start anything new while I was on the staff, the presbytery was still very much engaged in the questions of how young communities of worship and witness are sustained over time. And we did charter the community of Ghanaian immigrants who have since started another congregation! So when I began the work of coordinating the 1001 New Worshiping Communities movement of the Presbyterian Church (USA), I was not surprised that helping these new faith communities "figure out sustainability" quickly rose to the top of my To Do list. In fact, efforts to write this book had already begun under the leadership of my predecessor, Vera

White. The pages that follow are the result of a collaboration she imagined, and we are grateful for her vision.

Since the summer of 2012, when the General Assembly of the Presbyterian Church (USA) set the goal of starting 1001 new worshipping communities over a ten-year period, courageous leaders and risk-taking presbyteries along with faithful and curious partner congregations have launched well over 600 new worshipping communities. In addition to robust resources to support these starts, the Presbyterian Mission Agency has commissioned a longitudinal study of these communities and their leaders in hopes of learning everything we can from them. I commend to you the Annual Leaders Studies which can be found here: www.presbyterianmission.org/resources/topics/1001-2.

In addition to these reports, in 2019, we began specific research into the markers of sustainability in new worshipping communities through both qualitative and quantitative inquiries. Those investigations are ongoing and involve a comparison of communities launched with the resources and support of this current movement compared to previous models of starting new churches in the PC(USA). Our initial findings suggest communities with strong external support (from the presbytery and partner congregations) and leaders who take advantage of coaching and training opportunities are living longer than communities without this critical backing. However, we are not finding a perfect formula for success. Perhaps we are still in the process of identifying the most helpful questions to ask . . . which is where this book and these colleagues contribute invaluable insight.

Sustaining Grace offers the church the wise and prophetic voices of theologians, church planters, seminary faculty, presbytery leaders, and innovative pastors of inherited congregations engaged in the vital conversation of sustainability and impact in the whole ecosystem of the church. To mix a metaphor, the result is a rich and flavorful stew in which the youngest and oldest communities among us contribute the deep marrow of a complex broth and the fresh, bright herbs that take a bowl from basic comfort food to a delightful experience of hope. I give thanks and am encouraged by their reflections and am challenged by their prophetic questions.

To serve among these thinkers and to walk with these disciples is the great gift of this ministry.

Thank you, Barry, Jeya, Kristine, David, Michael, Aisha, and Beth, for forwarding our understanding of what a sustainable new church (and old church) might be. And thank you, Scott, Karen, and Michael, for bringing this book to fruition with your deep insight and powerful questions. Your work, on the wings of the Spirit, carries us forward.

Nikki Collins
Coordinator
1001 New Worshiping Communities

Acknowledgments

THIS BOOK MAKES THE case that the seemingly disparate communities that comprise the church need one another to flourish. The process of creating this book served to unearth that thesis in our lived experience.

This book began in April of 2018 with a group convened by the Church Planting Initiative of Pittsburgh Theological Seminary and the 1001 New Worshiping Communities program of the Presbyterian Church (USA). The group included church planters, pastors of established churches, seminary professors, mid-council leadership, and representatives from denominational agencies. The group was tasked to wrestle with the challenges of sustainability faced by many worshipping communities regardless of age. Each came with essays for the group to consider. They were the starting point for forty-eight hours of rich dialogue, and the raw material that would become the content of this book. We are grateful to each of the contributing authors, and trust that you, too, will appreciate their deep theological thinking, creative dreaming, and hard-earned wisdom. We are also grateful to Shawna Bowman, Raymond Bonwell, and Derrick Weston, who all participated in these initial conversations and contributed valuable insights that shaped our thinking and moved our conversation forward. Their contributions are echoed in the pages that follow.

Pittsburgh Theological Seminary hosted the initial conversation that led to this book. The Presbyterian Mission Agency and the Presbyterian Foundation provided substantial funding. For this and all the good work these institutions do for the church, we are grateful.

Vera White helped to envision this idea, and was catalytic in identifying and inviting the contributing participants. We also received significant support and encouragement from Nikki Collins, and administrative expertise from Eva Slayton. Thank you!

We give thanks to Jessa Darwin for doing much detail work to ensure the quality of this book, and to our partners at Wipf & Stock for providing a platform for this work to be shared.

Lastly, we give glory to our God, the Source of the church's sustaining grace.

1

Sustaining Grace

Innovative Ecosystems for New Faith Communities

SCOTT J. HAGLEY

IN ONE OF THE opening scenes of *Brother Sun, Sister Moon* (1972), the son of a wealthy medieval textile merchant, when offered the family business, instead strips off his brightly colored clothes and walks naked through the streets of his hometown of Assisi. Courageous, devoted, and incredibly vulnerable, the film captures what will become the parabolic power of medieval mendicant movements. This figure whom we know as St. Francis of Assisi took public and prophetic action, visibly protesting the trappings of wealth and the economic assumptions that promote it. The film wants us to see that the rest of his ministry was the natural extension of this initial act. St. Francis and those devoted to his way lived lives of radical dependence upon the generosity of others, demonstrating in their vulnerability the surprising abundance of medieval economic life and the scarcity experienced by those groaning under economic oppression.

It is not as though St. Francis demonstrates a way of life offered to everyone. He did, in the end, put clothes back on that were made, presumably, by a textile merchant. Gifts of shelter, money, and food were generously offered by those who made a living making, building, buying, and selling in the emerging economies of medieval Europe. And yet, the Franciscan presence signals the contradictions of economic life. Money cannot buy love or meaning, and its circulation threatens to corrupt whatever it touches, but we also cannot do without it. Francis can march naked in protest, but eventually he has to wear something and draw an income from somewhere.

Creative and transformative movements often make their home in the invisible contradictions of an era. They do not always display a universal path through various social tensions, but rather raise questions, create discomfort, and agitate for new dreams to emerge. Parabolic and prophetic actions function as a means of grace within cultures and social ecologies deadened by ideological boredom.

While perhaps not a new mendicant movement—innovative, entrepreneurial church leaders across the United States often find themselves in their own St. Francis moment. The statistics on mainline protestant church attendance are well known to denominational leaders and an experiential reality for churchgoers. Yet, in many of our denominations, our most promising leaders have shirked the mantle of nostalgia and imagined a different kind of future for mainline Christianity. In systems that assume particular economic and cultural capital for ordained ministry, pioneering leaders are cultivating Christian communities bi-vocationally, on shoestring budgets, and sometimes without theological education and a clerical collar. In denominations rich in real estate and endowments, these leaders are imagining church communities meeting in homes or third spaces, even envisioning repurposed church buildings as community centers.

By shedding comfortable religious structures and forms, these church leaders make themselves a compelling and provocative presence. On the one hand, they visibly protest the trappings of white, mainline civil religion. As new faith communities meet in living rooms, pubs, and elementary school gymnasiums, their energy and activism draws attention to the internal contradictions of denominational systems that protest social inequalities while drawing down endowment funds to maintain functionally empty heritage buildings. On the other hand, the vulnerability of such emerging communities makes them dependent upon whatever coaching, funds, benefits, and insurance such denominational systems can offer. But, as with St. Francis, these new leaders—and the communities they cultivate—are a means of grace for their reluctant denominational systems. Their presence punctures the ideological boredom of mainline religion, provoking new possibilities and dreams for Christian community in the United States; and yet their prophetic status makes them vulnerable and uncomfortably related to the denominational systems that need them.

Let me state my thesis as clearly as possible: American Mainline denominational systems *need* pioneering, adaptive leaders to experiment with new forms of Christian community, to dream a new shape for Christian identity in our present context. So also, pioneering, adaptive leaders *need* mainline denominational systems to provide the support that might make their work sustainable over the long haul. A creative space is opened by this contradiction: those setting aside the nostalgic covering of legacy congregations need the continuity and security these congregations provide, at the same time, legacy congregations need to learn to dream new dreams. This book explores the dynamic between new church development and denominational ecologies from the perspective of stewardship and sustainability. As a collection, the following essays suggest that in order to facilitate ecologies for missional innovation in post-Christendom, established congregations and new worshipping communities must image the sustaining grace of God to one another. Thus, problems of sustainability are not for church planters to solve alone, rather they are related to the theologies of stewardship and the ecclesial interconnections of the systems to which they belong.

This theme of sustaining grace emerged from a three-day writers' conference at Pittsburgh Theological Seminary in April of 2018. With generous funding from 1001 New Worshipping

Communities (NWC) and the Presbyterian Foundation, the Reverends Karen Rohrer and Michael Gehrling, and I convened a group of thirteen church planters, academics, and judicatory leaders from around the United States to work together on the question of stewardship and sustainability for New Worshipping Communities. While genuine differences exist and remain between the participants, we discovered in our conversation the ecological dimensions of these questions: sustainable, faithful work in church planting requires a holistic approach, imagining congregations as imaging God's sustaining grace to one another. In what follows, I will unpack this insight to introduce this book and its themes.

A "Mixed Economy" for Our New Missional Era

On the opening pages of *The End of White Christian America*, Robert P. Jones describes the elevator ride to the observation deck of One World Trade Center. While tourists ascend to the platform, a time-lapse video displays the transformation of Manhattan from a colonial outpost to the steel-and-glass skyline it is today. Up until the twentieth century, St. Paul's Chapel and Trinity Church were the most noticeable and pronounced structures dotting the Manhattan skyline. As the timeline moves toward the present day, however, these tall-steeple churches are dwarfed and eventually rendered invisible as churches are "eclipsed architecturally and culturally by commercial centers."[1] Throughout much of American history, White Protestantism claimed cultural power and prominence. The various adaptations of Protestant Christianity—from early evangelical revivals to the consolidation of mainline ecumenism and the emergence of neo-evangelicalism in the second half of the twentieth century—could claim a significant moral and public voice. But this era has passed with as much speed and discombobulation as a patched-together time-lapse video.

We mostly talk about these shifts in the negative. It is the *end* of an era; we are now *post*-Christian or *post*-Christendom or

1. Jones, *End of White Christian America*, 6.

post-modern. Such terms describe a liminal space. We know we have left one reality, but we have no idea how to talk about the new one. Such terms, however, unnecessarily problematize cultural change and suggest the problem with Mainline Protestantism is one of relevance. Our society has shifted away from Christianity, these terms suggest, and so we need to change in order to claim our rightful place in American public life. But what if the point is not to return to some era of hegemony, but rather to discover the shape of Christian faithfulness within this "new missional era"?[2] What if the *missio Dei* invites us into a different kind of public witness than the one previously enjoyed by Mainline Protestantism? New worshipping communities often lead such discovery, helping us to navigate the basic elements—soil, air, water, and shelter—of our new missional era.

The Soil We Cultivate: The "Disestablishment" of the Church

Churches in the United States have had to learn to cultivate Christian life in the soil of religious disestablishment. For denominations descended from European state-churches, like Lutheran, Presbyterian, and Episcopalian, the United States provides a different kind of social and political context for religious practice and expression. The legal separation of church and state has created a tumultuous and creative religious economy, where ecclesiastical bodies must learn to operate without the security and authority provided by a political entity.[3] Upstart movements like the Methodists in the nineteenth century, and Baptists and Mormons in the twentieth have shaped the American context in ways not seen in Western Europe or even, to a lesser extent, Canada. The church in America has always had to grow in the soil of disestablishment.

2. I borrow this term from Pat Keifert, who uses it to reframe post-Christendom in *We Are Here Now*.

3. See Finke and Stark, *Churching of America*. See also Van Gelder, "Ecclesial Geno-Project," 12–45.

"Disestablishment" names not a singular legal arrangement structured by the First Amendment, but rather a peculiar way in which religious practice and organization has taken shape in the United States. In Colonial New England, the Puritans enjoyed cultural, political, and religious hegemony until the field preaching of George Whitefield and the First Great Awakening. Prioritizing individual decision and personal piety, Whitefield's preaching undermined the social arrangements and the ecclesial imagination that sustained Puritan and Anglican establishments.[4] This prioritization of the individual has as much to do with the shape of American religious practice as the separation of church and state. Most Christian communities in the United States embody some commitment to individual choice and voluntary participation. Americans largely choose their Christian faith, regardless of polity or theologies of baptism.

Besides revivalism and the constitutional protections for a pluralist public sphere, an increasingly diverse and morally fragmented population also creates a sense of religious disestablishment. Throughout the twentieth and twenty-first centuries, the United States has become more religiously diverse. We hear a lot about the "Nones" and "Dones" in relationship to Christianity, but we hear less about American Muslim, Hindu, and Buddhist communities in our cities. In many ways, both Mainline and Evangelical Christian communities are unprepared for faith formation in these new pluralist public spaces. Yet, like soil turned over in a garden, the present uncertainty of Mainline and Evangelical congregations in majority cultures is consistent with the ongoing processes of disestablishment representative of the American context. This is one reason why, in movements like 1001 New Worshipping Communities of the Presbyterian Church (USA) (PC[USA]), the constitution and leadership of new worshipping communities are much more diverse than the denomination as a whole.

4. Noll, *Old Religion in a New World*, 52.

The Air We Breathe: Our "Secular Age"

At the beginning of *A Secular Age*, Canadian philosopher Charles Taylor asks why, over the past five hundred years, Western societies have shifted away from theistic assumptions.[5] Previously, the burden of proof fell on those who imagined a world without God, whereas now those who believe in God must offer reasons for their commitment. In making this comparison, Taylor articulates the background conditions of contemporary religious belief.[6] Modern secularism is not really about the decline of the church or the subtraction of religion from public life. Rather, it is one way of describing the modern social imaginary. Our *age* is secular, in that we generally and easily imagine the world without divine agency. Secularity is, simply put, the air we breathe.

Taylor's work offers at least two advantages for understanding the challenges of Christian worship and witness in the contemporary world. First, Taylor makes visible the new conditions under which Christians experience Christian commitment and faith. In our secular age, we hold Christian commitments against a backdrop of other possibilities and competing claims. For example, when I claim that God exists, or that God sustains all that exists, I do so fully conscious of competing claims and aware that such claims place upon me a certain burden of proof. That is, even when I discuss God's work in the world, I can imagine—and know people of goodwill who envision—a world without God's active agency. As Craig Gay has said, the structures, practices, and imaginary of the modern world make it "easy to live in a world where God does not exist."[7] Second, the story Taylor tells makes it clear that such a world is a partial, though unexpected, accomplishment of Western Christendom. Our secular age does not come from outside Western theological and intellectual traditions, but

5. See Taylor, *Secular Age*.

6. Taylor uses the term "conditions of belief" to talk about his focus, though James K. A. Smith uses the metaphor of "background" to talk about Taylor's concern. See Smith, *How Not to Be Secular*, 18.

7. Gay, *Way of the (Modern) World*, 338.

is rather a manifestation of certain impulses toward equality, individual agency, and moral consistency. The air we breathe may provide certain challenges to ecclesial formation, but it is not altogether hostile or corrupt; it simply *is*. The church in a secular age must learn to breathe *this* air.

The Water We Drink: The End of Congregationalism

Mission historians sometimes describe the years between 1792 and 1914 as "the Great Century of missions."[8] In 1792, the Baptist Shoemaker William Carey wrote *An Enquiry*, where he draws a comparison between the capital-raising and focused organization of corporations like the Hudson Bay Company and Jesus' command to "go into all the nations" in Matthew 28. And 1914, of course, refers to the "Great War," which brought missionary cooperation and notions of Western moral supremacy to a cataclysmic halt. Between these dates, a burst of missionary activism emanated from Western nations through the technology developed by Carey and others: the voluntary missionary society (VMS). As imagined by Carey and his contemporaries, the VMS provided a means for the "fortunate subversion of the church" as it provided a technology for like-minded Christians to organize themselves for the sake of mission apart from denominational and ecclesial hierarchies.[9] It is, as Andrew Walls says, "one of God's theological jokes" played on those church-people who imagined themselves as holding the keys to ecclesial expression.[10]

In the United States, the VMS coincided with Western expansion and religious competition. As mentioned above, religious disestablishment made room for creative and entrepreneurial ministries in America's cities and on the frontier. Such conditions

8. Many describe the era this way. The most authoritative account comes from Kenneth Scott Latourette's seven-volume series The Expansion of Christianity. See Latourette, *Great Century*, vol. 4, *Europe and the United States*; as well as Latourette, *Great Century*, vol. 5, *The Americas, Australasia, and Africa.*

9. See Walls, *Missionary Movement in Christian History*, 241–54.

10. Walls, *Missionary Movement in Christian History*, 246.

made the VMS a natural mode for religious mobilization and activism. Christians in the United States organized not only for missions overseas, but also for mission on the frontier. The voluntary society was invented in Europe, but it was perfected in the United States. Spread across a vast territory and supported by networks of like-minded Christians, one consequence of the "great century" of missions is the creation of a distinct form of American Christianity that is at once entrepreneurial, activistic, and individualistic.[11]

In this way, voluntarism and the structures that make voluntary associations possible nourished the growth of American Christianity. Indeed, it is difficult to imagine how congregations can form and function apart from voluntary principles and ways of organization. This is the water we drink. Because of our long history with voluntary societies, we imagine congregations as voluntary associations—even when our polity says otherwise. We choose a congregation based on how it fits our needs and we sustain congregations through voluntary giving.

However, this well of nourishment seems to be drying up. Voluntarism has been in decline for decades in the United States.[12] Neighborhood associations and community organizations struggle to find both support and plausibility in the modern world. With declining participation in these organizations, congregational life—with its committees, dependence upon voluntary giving, and idiosyncratic elements of common life—is sometimes difficult to maintain. As one friend of mine often says, congregations are performing their programs at a higher level than ever before, but with decreasing results. The great century of missions may have ended a hundred years ago, but congregations in the United States are just starting to feel its consequences.

11. Walls, *Missionary Movement in Christian History*, 221–40

12. See Putnam, "Tuning In, Tuning Out," 664–83. Sociologists continue to debate the reasons for this decline, with some recent studies suggesting that Putnam's reading of the data obscures the *episodic* nature of volunteering in contemporary society. People still volunteer, but they do so with less consistency with a singular organization over time. Either way, it signals a shift in the social fabric that congregations depend upon. See Rotolo and Wilson, "What Happened to the 'Long Civic Generation'?," 1091–121.

With the rise of trans-global Pentecostal movements, as outlined in *The Rise of Network Christianity*, and in movements toward localism and asset-based community development, it seems as though we may be entering a post-congregational era for the church in the United States.[13] The well from which we have been nourished is running dry. Where, then, might we turn for nourishment? What new social arrangements and movements can help Christians to cultivate community in this post-congregationalist and post-voluntarist age?

The House We Have Inherited: Crumbling Structures of Christendom

In many ways, "Post-Christendom" signals, as Robert P. Jones has said, the "end of White Christian America." White Mainline Protestants and Evangelicals have operated within a general assumption of cultural and political power. But this cultural hegemony has come at a cost; the *form* of Christianity inherited from Europe and situated within the majority cultures of the United States, has carried the virus and full-fledged disease of racism and white supremacy.[14] Beyond tacit and direct support for slavery and Jim Crow, White Protestant Mainline and Evangelical Christianity inherited from Europe both the tribal loyalties that constituted Christendom and the dualisms of the Enlightenment.

13. "Post-congregational" signals a possible shift in how people participate in religious community apart from some of the traditional elements of congregational organization. *The Rise of Network Christianity* names one way, where people still depend upon large congregations and conferences for resourcing and inspiration, but then self-organize in surprising ways for ministry and mission. In other quarters of the North American church, books like *The New Parish* name a different kind of framework for Christian community—pointing toward neighborhood-focused ministry which may or may exist between or apart from congregations. See Christerson and Flory, *Rise of Network Christianity*. See also Sparks et al., *New Parish*.

14. Several scholars have meticulously documented the theological roots of white supremacy and racial ideologies. See, for example, Carter, *Race: A Theological Account*. See also Jennings, *Christian Imagination*.

In the first case, Andrew Walls and others understand the origins of Christendom, not in the conversion of Constantine, but in the conversion of the pagan tribes of Northern Europe, where missionaries focused their attention on the loyalties of kings and royalty, with the aim to convert an entire people.[15] For Germanic and Scandinavian peoples, religious, geographic, political, and cultural realms were integrated into a unified whole. A ruler united subjects through religious loyalty; conversions were thus holistic and territorial. Within the cultural imagination of Christendom, expansive visions of the missionary movement, such as when Pope Alexander VI divides the world between Spain and Portugal or when William Carey extensively charts the known religious beliefs of the entire world, are extensions of the Euro-tribal integration between people, land, culture, politics, and religion. The power of European nations over other peoples could be imagined religiously, even *Christianly*, within the narrative framework of Christendom. Mission was thus seen as *expansion* and benevolence, an act of power and obligation.

But, according to Jehu Hanciles, it is precisely this expansion that exposes the limitations of a Euro-tribal faith.[16] As European influence spread, the Christendom faith was under-equipped for its encounter with pluralist forms of Christianity and pluralist religious spaces. New Christian communities on non-European soil introduced surprising innovations and questions into the Christian practice and identity. Questions around polygamy, evil spirits, or ancestor veneration, which seemed settled to missionaries, were suddenly cracked open again with nuance and challenges not anticipated by Western missionaries. Under the strains of such questions, the notion of a homogenous geographic, political, and cultural Christian identity proved implausible. Similarly, Christendom theologies and ecclesial practices have proved inadequate to the challenges posed by interreligious contexts. Ecclesiologies formed in relationship to cultural and political privilege must

15. Walls, *Missionary Movement in Christian History*, 26–42, 68–75. See also Hanciles, *Beyond Christendom*, 84–111.

16. Hanciles, *Beyond Christendom*, 84–111.

undergo significant transformation to function in settings of religious persecution or as a religious minority. Christian identity is formed differently in religiously plural contexts, as churches in the West continue to discover. In some ways, we might say that the success of European mission in catalyzing indigenous communities undermined the very conditions under which the Euro-tribal faith was formed. The Euro-tribal faith appears implausible amid this pluralist reality and world Christianity.

Willie Jennings identifies in the above narrative the "diseased social imagination" of the West, which manifests itself in racial ideologies, racism, and White supremacy.[17] In Jennings' telling, Western missionaries, armies, and businesses moved across great distances without attentiveness to place and locality. Western peoples intended to put their mark on foreign landscapes, people, cultures, and languages; they translated texts into vernacular languages, educated indigenous peoples in the catechisms of Western Europe, subjected whole communities to the self-serving force field of global trade, and remade the world. The shores upon which Westerners landed were imagined as wide open spaces for the imposition of Western will and order: what we still tend to imagine with a word like "frontier." While coercive and oppressive, such actions also betray deeper "dislocative" and "dis-associative" postures in Western Christianity.[18] The truly local, cultural, and embodied elements of Western Christian identity were universalized and extended in a way that obscured the beauty and goodness of local practices, people, economies, and ways of life. Of course, mission history also registers voices of complaint and prophetic critique. But these voices only clarify the coercive dislocative and dis-associative habits of Western Christianity.

This is the house we have inherited within denominations that descend from European soil in the United States. Our theological traditions, ecclesial practices, and cultural discourses come to us from within the structures of Christendom. When congregations imagine themselves as a lone beacon of light in a dark

17. Jennings, *Christian Imagination*, 6.

18. Jennings, *Christian Imagination*, 7.

neighborhood, or take upon themselves the task of dispensing wisdom and resources to and for a community, they disclose the very dis-associative and dislocative postures of Western Christianity. When the political arms of our various denominations imagine "taking back our country" (whether on the right or the left) or when we imagine witness as a kind of expansion, we pull the veil back just a bit to reveal our Euro-tribal heritage. But, as both Hanciles and Jennings can attest, this house is crumbling, rotting from within by its own internal contradictions. The pluralist and interconnected world made by the missionary, soldier, and merchant is one that finds Euro-tribal Christianity increasingly implausible. A pluralist world Christianity begs for Christian identity to be formed in dynamic interaction with local contexts, and in partnership with others.

Cultivating the Soil, Air, and Water; Picking through the Ruins

Garfield Community Farm sits atop the neighborhood for which it is named on three derelict blocks in the city of Pittsburgh. In the decades after steel mills closed and "white flight" gutted the city, whole blocks of homes were torn down in Garfield, leaving a visible scar of the region's economic and racial dysfunction. In the middle of the last century, the neighborhood was known as a garden community. Topographically separated from the noise and traffic of the commercial district at the bottom of the hill, fruit-bearing trees lined the streets of Garfield, kids played in the streets, and multigenerational families occupied the row houses and duplexes in the community. At present, Garfield shows signs of such history. Families still raise children in the neighborhood, residents still tend gardens in their front yard and look out for one another. But such activities are done amid the rubble of abandoned homes, impassible streets, occasional outbursts of violence, and overgrown, untended green spaces.

Over seven years ago, members from two churches in the neighborhood began to work one of these untended green spaces where row houses once stood. Cutting back Japanese knot weed and clearing the brush that had grown up over the foundations of demolished buildings, volunteers began cultivating the topsoil and creating plots to grow vegetables. The work was difficult and adaptive. Water needed to be siphoned from the city's water main or collected in rain barrels; decades of neglect and pollution had taken its toll on the soil, which did not yield growth in the early years; weeds and groundhogs did not easily relinquish their grip on the ecosystem. But the fledgling work inspired others and gained partners in the neighborhood and across the city. Slowly the land has been cultivated, the soil enriched, and a community green space repurposed for the neighborhood. Fruit-bearing trees, chickens, ducks, hops, and a wide array of indigenous vegetables and plants now grow at the farm under the water tower. Families now work and children play again in this space. The material conditions of the neighborhood have been cultivated in such a way that new life has emerged in the midst of ruins.

Many of our church communities and systems are no longer thriving. We have found ourselves on difficult soil, breathing unfamiliar air, looking for a new water source, and inhabiting condemned structures rotting from the inside. Recent decades have seen many creative attempts to engage these shifts. We have doubled down on program-oriented churches, seeking to resource ministries to be more attractive and "seeker-sensitive." We have seen the rise of so-called megachurches, who provide concert-quality Sunday morning experiences. We have drunk deeply from the well of leadership theory, sharpening our systems and increasing our efficiency. But, while many of these efforts are good in their own way, they are largely attempts to recover a past rather than imagine a future. And, like attempting to rebuild a dilapidated row house with crumbling materials, the effort offers diminishing returns.

The problem is that we fail to recognize these various elements of "Post-Christendom" as naming for us a new missional era for the church. We fail to consider what God might be up to in our midst. Perhaps God invites Mainline Christians to reconsider narratives of expansion and benevolence. Perhaps the sudden vulnerability experienced by Mainline and Evangelical churches carries with it the provocative and disruptive Word of God. Perhaps the task for churches in the United States is to neither challenge nor acquiesce to our secular age, but to discover faithful means to witness to the gospel of Jesus Christ within it. Perhaps the ongoing disestablishment of the church offers a gift to those communities raised on the expectation of privilege and hegemony. Perhaps the work for our judicatories and congregations looks more like Garfield Farm.

Mission, in other words, shifts our attention from *conflict with* the dimensions of earth, air, water, and shelter mentioned above to *discovery within* these realities of contemporary life. In 1952 the International Missionary Council met in Willingen, Germany, around the question "Why Missions?" The council was wrestling with its own plausibility in light of many of the trends described above. Independence movements in the global south, ongoing trauma after the Second World War, and suspicion that "missions" and "colonialism" were bound up with each other rightly led to a crisis of identity. The council never came to a clear agreement regarding a specific proposal, but it did rediscover a theological framework that has become a kind of "Copernican revolution" in mission theology.[19] In its engagement with Barthian theology and a renewed interest in Trinitarian discourse, the council document entitled *Missions under the Cross* called attention to a *theocentric* understanding of mission: *missio Dei*.[20] God, the council affirmed, is both the agent and the end of mission. In subsequent decades this discovery has generated a theocentric rationale for congregational identity and ministry. God calls, equips, and sends God's people into the world, not for the sake of growing congregations or extending influence, but rather so that such people might *encounter* and *witness* the reconciling work of God in Jesus Christ. Because

19. Van Gelder, "How Missiology Can Help," 20.

20. The council document provided a launching point for a theology of the *missio Dei*, but did not necessarily develop the theology. See Flett, *Witness of God*, 123–62.

the Triune God is the agent and end of mission, the church in the United States is to go out into this new terrain with the expectation and hope that we will encounter the triune *missio Dei* amid the ruins of our failing structures offering gifts that cultivate new life, gifts like earth, water, and air.

For the most part, those who form new Christian communities already understand this. Sometimes church planting works like the opening up of a new franchise, where a prepackaged worship experience is launched in a new building or neighborhood. But increasingly, church planting engages the slow, relational, and adaptive work of joining a particular community, working creatively with the cultural and social materials in that place, and discerning a shape of life and form of witness attentive to these dynamics. And, like the work of Garfield Farm, church planting in this slow, relational, and *missional* way requires a dense network of support: relational, emotional, spiritual, and financial. Because these communities are vulnerable and costly, many judicatories offer training, coaching, and grants to fund the early years of church development. In doing this, we assume that these new communities *need* the support of the judicatory for a short time until they can become "self-sustaining."

What we often fail to recognize is how much our judicatories need church planters, whether or not their projects ever become self-sustaining. Our new missional era presents our church systems with a massive adaptive challenge, which cannot be avoided or ignored. New congregations and experiments in Christian community teach us what it looks like to engage these challenges in faith and hope rather than fear and nostalgia. For this reason, we cannot separate the question of sustainability for new churches from the larger question of sustainability for our judicatories and ecclesial systems. We need an ecological, or a "mixed economy," approach to questions of sustainability for the sake of church innovation and discovery in our new missional era.[21]

The Fresh Expressions movement in the Church of England began using the term "mixed economy" to talk about the

21. Cray, *Mission-Shaped Church*, vii.

relationship between "fresh expressions" churches, which were often formed around subcultures and interest groups, and congregations organized according to the parish model.[22] "Mixed economy" communicates the value of both forms of church organization; the system can tolerate and even thrive with a broad range of approaches to ministry and mission. In the case of Fresh Expressions, this has not only served a rhetorical purpose, but has generated open-ended creativity. The missiological challenges faced by the Church of England require an ecosystem that can encourage creativity and innovation while simultaneously tending to historic and legacy congregations.

While the United States context is notably different from the United Kingdom, and not all polities permit the kind of organization exhibited by the Church of England, the metaphor remains apt. The "new missional era" of the twenty-first-century United States requires an ecological approach to innovation and revitalization.

Signs of Life: Ecologies of Ecclesial Innovation

Right before the stones start to rain down on Stephen, he utters one of the central themes that drive the Acts narrative: "The Most High does not dwell in houses made with human hands."[23] Indeed, Stephen's whole speech evokes a comparison with the resurrection narratives: "Why do you look for the living among the dead? He is not here, but has risen. . . ."[24] The Acts narrative drives this point home. God is not always at work where we expect. God is the Living One not contained by the structures we have constructed to understand and worship the Divine. Of course, this places a community that witnesses to the Resurrected Christ on precarious ground. We must build "houses," or systems and structures to organize our shared life, and yet the boundaries we draw and the

22. Cray, *Mission-Shaped Church*, 1–28

23. Acts 7:48 NRSV.

24. Luke 24:5 NRSV.

commitments we make are subject to the presence and action of God in Jesus Christ and through the Holy Spirit.

Luke's paradigmatic example of this reality is in Acts 10–11, where Peter is called by the Spirit to the house of Cornelius, a God-fearing Gentile and centurion in the Roman army. The encounter transforms both Cornelius and Peter. Cornelius receives the gift of the Holy Spirit and is baptized into the fellowship of the community of Christ; Peter discovers God's acceptance of Gentiles *as Gentiles*. This discovery raises substantive and distressing questions for the early faith community. It eventually makes Christianity a religion capable of dramatic cultural translation and diversity. The inclusion of Gentiles into the early Christian community reflects a type of innovation that is both theological and structural. Jews and Gentiles had to figure out how to be in community with each other. The Acts narrative identifies something central to Christian community over the centuries. Whenever Christianity crosses ethnic, cultural, linguistic, or geographic boundaries, it requires all parties involved to learn new things. This is one implication of a resurrected Lord. Innovation is not just paramount to mission, it is a critical feature of Christian faithfulness.

As a collection, the essays offered in this book suggest an ecological, "mixed economy" approach to the question of innovation in our new missional era. Drawing from church planters, theologians, and judicatory leaders, we identify the provocative presence that church planting provides within judicatory systems. Like Francis walking naked through the streets of Assisi, or like Peter coming back to Jerusalem with the scent of unclean foods on his clothing, experiments in Christian community generate questions, surprise us, disturb us, and help us to identify new possibilities for God's presence and work in our midst. The profound depth of the challenges we face will require us to innovate in relationship to God's mission. Beginning with this assumption, we intend to encourage ecologies for ecclesial innovation. These ecologies will need to do several things.

First, those interested in cultivating ecologies for ecclesial innovation need to think systemically and ecologically about sustainability. Stewardship campaigns are not enough. We need systems that can institutionalize the ways in which legacy and new church developments need one another. As a start, we should interrogate the value of "self-sustaining" as an immediate goal for new faith communities. In chapter 2, Karen Rohrer, Director of the Church Planting Initiative at Pittsburgh Theological Seminary, describes the institutional and financial challenges church planters face, in order to suggest one way that church systems can support the work of church planting in a concrete way. Barry Ensign-George, who is the Coordinator for Theology and Worship at the Presbyterian Mission Agency, offers in the third chapter an institutional perspective on the question of sustainability, exploring the necessary tension between maintenance and dynamic experimentation within institutions. What does it mean that communities across denominational systems need one another? And Scott Hagley, Associate Professor of Missiology at Pittsburgh Theological Seminary, considers questions of stewardship and sustainability within the practices and liturgies of consumer capitalism in chapter 4.

Second, stewardship campaigns may not be enough, but sustaining ecologies of innovation will require practices that form and inform faithful and sustained leaders to do the work of new and inherited faith communities. Michael Gehrling, Associate for Assessment and Northeast Region for 1001 NWC, reminds us in chapter 5 of the need to hear and welcome feedback and highlights the practices of openness so often present in new faith community leadership that make for agile and sustainable faithfulness. In chapter 6, Aisha Brooks-Lytle, Executive Presbyter of the Greater Atlanta Presbytery, explores the many languages and practices of prayer, gleaned from the broader church, cultivated by, and needed for leadership in the diversity of possibilities in the new missional era. Kristine Stache, Associate Professor of Missional Ministry at Wartburg Seminary, reminds us in chapter 7 of the way the roles we play comprise our vocations, their boundaries shape our faithfulness, and the diverse ecosystems of our lives and congregations invite us into the improvisation of faithfulness here and now. And in chapter 8, David Loleng, Director of Church Financial Literacy and Leadership at the Presbyterian Foundation, suggests a shift away from stewardship programs and toward spiritual disciplines that teach generosity and gratitude.

Third, ecologies of innovation offer creative spaces for leadership development and ongoing care. In the ninth chapter, Michael Moynah, Director of Network Development for Fresh Expression, UK, considers the importance of extending stewardship and sustainability conversations to practices and processes for leadership development. Beth Scibienski, pastor of Grace Presbyterian Church, describes in chapter 10 her own experience directing a congregation's stewardship efforts from a concern for self-sustainability toward sharing its gifts for the good of the broader community. And finally, Jeya So, founding co-pastor of Anchor City Church, describes in chapter 11 the surprising dimensions of leadership development in her own congregation, where the emerging gifts of her community continue to challenge traditional leadership motifs and expectations.

Through Jesus Christ and in the Holy Spirit, God invites us to participate in the triune *missio Dei*. The conversations that gave rise to this book brought a breadth of experiences, concerns, and hard-won wisdom to the table. We write this volume with the kind of hope one discovers at the empty tomb or while encountering a stranger on the road to Emmaus. We who are planting churches and who are leading congregations, we who are teaching classes or serving on judicatory committees are, in the end, co-participants with each other in this good work. May we learn to see in one another God's sustaining grace.

Section 1

Sustainable Ecologies for New Church Development

2

A Small Shift toward Sharing All Things in Common

Karen Rohrer

In the Belief Series Commentary on Acts, Willie Jennings reads the story of Ananias and Saphira - the couple who sells land, lies to the community about the price they got for it, attempts to keep the remainder for themselves, and dies - as dismantling the idolatry of the couple in the early church. After engaging the intensity of such a story, the very real violence undertaken by the Holy Spirit, and thus the disallowing of the community from enacting such violence themselves, Jennings explores how the economics Ananias and Sapphira practiced as a couple reflect their notion that the couple is primary, and that the gathered community of Jesus followers exists to serve the couple, rather than the other way around. Jennings goes on to explore how in the West, this view of the couple has been entrenched as a cultural value. From there, he calls on Christians to end "the heresy that the couple is the only safe and sanctioned place where the honesty, safety, and joy of being vulnerable creatures may be touched and celebrated."[1] In the text of Acts 5, Jennings sees a God who is disrupting that hegemony,

1. Jennings, *Commentary on Acts*, 58.

opening up community to the broad scope of God's desire for God's people at work with and among them, and restoring the couple to its rightful place in service to the larger community. The story is one of in-breaking, disrupting, and enacted re-visioning of what it means to be the community of Jesus followers.

The commentary left me wondering if, perhaps, we have followed the same pattern of idolizing couples that Jennings describes—only in our idolization of the local congregation. In other words, could our understanding of the rightful role of our congregations be faithfully described as "the heresy that" *our congregation* "is the only safe and sanctioned place where the honesty, safety, and joy of being" *spiritual* "creatures may be touched and celebrated?" Indeed, there is good financial evidence, at least in the PC(USA), that we increasingly live as though the church is there for congregations rather than congregations being there for the church.[2] To put it in the language of this book—we are living as if the broader church ecosystem exists to serve each plant, rather than each plant serving the health of the larger church ecosystem. Because our local church is the space where we experience God most fully, it is easy to imagine that small stage as the most important setting for the work of God. But if we begin to think that our specific congregation is the most important thing in all our faith practices—a microcosm that can hold the whole of the church, just because it is the primary way *we personally* experience God in the world, then we end up in increasingly narrow communions, divesting resources from other gathered communities of Christ, and believing that we alone see God rightly. Could it be that, like Ananias and Sapphira, we are holding back money from the sale of some property, so that we in our congregation don't have to share the same frightening fate of the broader community of believers who may very well run out of money? Is it possible we are thinking to ourselves, even now, "But if they all run out of money and we still have our endowment left, then we will still be there to undertake the witness and work of the church"?

I am a little bit afraid we are.

2. Nelson, "Stated Clerk."

And I am afraid that I see different manifestations of that line of thinking throughout the congregational economic practices of my beloved home tradition, the PC(USA). So, recognizing that practices both reflect and shape the imagination of the practitioner, my hope for this essay is that together, we can imagine possibilities for our communities beyond the fear and self-preservation instincts of our Ananias and Sapphira culture.

Indeed, one of the gifts and challenges of the Ananias and Sapphira story is the seriousness with which it takes their economic practice within the community of believers. Somewhat shockingly, the Holy Spirit seems to see this kind of behavior (and presumably the assumptions behind such behavior) as a matter of life and death. Given this testimony, I am invited to consider where I myself most closely fit in the story. As I write this, I am in a warm office, with a humming heater, where I am paid a living wage and welcomed by a supportive community. It is currently under 26 degrees outside and three blocks away, my neighbors are going through metal detectors to spend time in a warm space and seek emergency support at East End Cooperative Ministry. In short, there should be no confusion about my role as a sort of Ananias/Sapphira-type figure.

As an ordained pastor, I make above the mandated presbytery minimum salary, while I know of several ordained pastors, particularly in new immigrant faith communities and new church starts, who do not—and I do not give the money back. As a congregant, I watch my congregation faithfully pay per capita, but live out of an endowment that is not necessarily tithed for the work of other faith communities in our city who might engage those we do not reach. In the midst of these simple failures to practice equity, I do not know how the vulnerable stand by and watch us church people do things like buy new carpet for the office wing while the children of their churches go hungry, the buildings we built in their communities go untended, and the injustices they face go unquestioned. And even as I am culpable, I think it is morally dangerous that I and we behave in that way—purposefully isolated from the suffering and humanity of others, in or outside of our churches.

My intention is not to pile personal guilt upon personal guilt, but rather to name the realities of life and death we live in, even in a prosperous context. As Jennings wisely points out, this heresy of placing self over community and insiders over outsiders is a cultural one, not just an individual one. So even in our own guilty hearts, amid our own guilty culture, we recognize what great help we will need, when we lean hard on our tradition, and assert with the Brief Statement of Faith that "the Spirit gives us courage . . . to unmask idolatries in Church and culture."[3]

We know that the call is not only to unmask idolatries, but to be changed by facing them, so that we imagine different community practices—even and especially the economic practices by which we live together. The call is to imagine different ways of living as congregations, animated by a vision not of how the church serves our local congregation, but how our local congregation serves the whole church as it lives its calling in community with the whole world.

The church cannot live its calling in community with the whole world if there are not churches in poor neighborhoods. The church cannot live in community with the whole world if there is not acceptance and recognition of indigenous expressions of the gospel around the world. The church cannot live in community with the world if what is needed for church is a certain amount of money or property or economic sustainability to meet the standard of church. The prophetic call to unmask idolatries must include the work of seeing and living another way.

Right now, the economic imagination we practice in our individual churches is governed by the business world. I will not argue that we should dispense with an economic imagination altogether, as we, with or without willing it, participate in and comprise economies all the time. Rather, I am arguing for a shift in our particular economic imagination. Our current business world imagination sees our life together as a set of programs run by a programmatic professional, a pastor, who can be paid to do

3. PC(USA), "Brief Statement of Faith," in *Constitution of the Presbyterian Church*, lines 66–69.

the things only he[4] knows how to do. This professional should be trained and prepared, experienced with the norms of a certain social class, and living in accordance with the values of a certain economic situation.[5] He is a professional paid for his service, the programs are a measure of his performance, and the outcomes of those programs over time are a clear articulation of his value. Because our guiding metaphor here is so informed by the business world, our interaction with pastors is profoundly economic, where salary, benefits, and housing are on one side of the table for conversation, with the other side being governed by productivity, programs, and their ability to persist and even gain ground and attendance over time.

By nature, businesses are self-contained and clearly bounded. The goal is value growth for shareholders with every other relationship subservient to that one. The shareholder bias, like Ananias and Sapphira's couple bias, quickly becomes an idol when it is lived in the church. Even in systems like the PC(USA), where the employer/employee relationship with leaders is bounded by salary minimums and provision of excellent benefits, imagining the relationship as a business relationship limits what is possible, both for the minister and the congregation. Not only does it limit the possibilities for the way a church does life together, it helps to create a structure that leads to the shareholder bias. The thought is, "We hired him so that he would produce this program and increase its reach *on our behalf*." Just that simple phrase signifies a dangerous shift of thinking.

4. I say "he" because the inherited churches of size and budget to be able to seek the sort of "professionals" I am describing, have, according to recent Board of Pensions data, generally chosen men as those professionals. See *Living the Gospel*. As a result, I will be using "he" pronouns throughout in reference to the "professional pastor." A different essay would be needed to fully explore the relationship between this sort of imagined economic model and the patriarchy that this data points to.

5. Some presbyteries even require credit checks of folks going through the ordination process—which is not to say that trustworthiness is not an appropriate standard for Ministers of Word and Sacrament but rather that one's credit score is a rather flawed, limited, and class-coded measure of one's trustworthiness.

Envisioning the pastor as providing a service to a congregation and accountable to a governing board presents a lot of issues, but is particularly problematic when the congregation is then in service to its individual members or shareholders, rather than in service to the broader church living out its calling in community with the world. In that schema, we end up with a church that is for the smallest possible constituency, a pastor who cannot possibly please everyone, and an external, broader church and world that are not considered or engaged at all. In light of all this, a reimagining of how power flows as pastors relate to the congregations they serve is essential to shift our vision and then our practiced life together within the system more broadly.

The Small Shift in Question

The world of starting new faith communities offers a space where such a shift might be possible, both because there is no institutional habit in place and because the work and ministry before the pastor in a new faith community is naturally quite different than that before the pastor of an inherited church. Not only that, but without congregational shareholders in place, the larger church (as often represented by a presbytery committee, at least in the PC[USA]) is often left to be the hiring and accountability structure, which places accountability more naturally within the broader ecosystem. As such, these representatives of the larger church have interests that are naturally placed in the broader ecosystem simply by virtue of sitting on a judicatory-wide committee invested in new communities. Additionally, their engagement is not as a consumer of one of those community's programs, but rather as participants in the larger system. The leader they seek to hire is also participating in a different incentive structure than those leaders pursuing work in inherited faith communities. The potential new leaders are those who are moved by risk and animated by care for those outside the church. Often, but not always, they are young leaders, recently out of seminary, and seeking to convene a faith community different from those they have encountered. Often, but not always, they are interested in caring for marginalized communities, sometimes because they are a member of one themselves. All these factors make new faith communities prime spaces for a new imagination and a new practice to take shape. And, because change is hard in large systems, and re-visioning is more easily done with examples before us, this space for change and experimentation in new faith communities also plays a role in risking on behalf of inherited churches, by serving as a space to engage and workshop new possibilities that could ultimately, once fully developed, be offered to the broader church.

Indeed, this can be one of the roles of new faith communities in and for the whole church. In keeping with the imaginative move to be for the full church, we must be careful to honor both new faith communities and inherited churches in the process of this shift. If new faith communities are to be employed to experiment on behalf of the broader system, it stands to reason that the larger system must be careful not to instrumentalize them simply for the benefit of other individual communities, but rather to treat them as partners in the work, so that neither the new community nor the planting leader is seen as disposable once their work proves informative to the larger body. Indeed, if this system is to reimagine congregations as finding their purpose in service to the church as it lives its calling in community with the whole world, then just as no communities should be idolized, so too, no communities should be instrumentalized or viewed as disposable. Again, health must be understood ecosystem wide, rather than something that can somehow be divided or parsed out.

Knowing that new faith communities are the place to attempt such reimagined practices, what potential practices might signify a commitment to partnership among leaders and communities who live out their ministries in different and distinct ways, offering different and distinct gifts back to the church, in service to the whole body? In other words, what practices might bring us closer to sharing all things in common across the broader church ecosystem, rather than channeling resources toward particularly well-heeled corners and using them only in service to more highly valued forms of community, just as Ananias and Sapphira did?

I submit a very specific practice for consideration in new faith communities: a $10,000 signing bonus for leaders called to convene those new faith communities. This funding would be valuable both literally and symbolically, and as such, should at least partially come from judicatory funds gleaned not from an endowment. Some portion should come from neighboring congregations as their risk in solidarity with communities beyond themselves (in the larger church), their risk in solidarity with constituencies they do not engage (in the world), and their risk in solidarity with the practiced faithfulness, learning, and experimentation that will infuse them as part of the larger ecosystem. Through the judicatory, these churches would be able to risk in solidarity with, but not directly benefit from, this new community. They would be able to feel the importance of both the community and its leader's thriving, while learning a new way to give that does not bring them direct reward or pay off in the ways to which they are accustomed. In this circumstance, they can honestly understand themselves as partners in solidarity, and clearly state their own role in practiced faithfulness, learning, and experimentation as both essential and indirect, giving them the freedom to live as keepers of the tradition, while still valuing and supporting the innovation others might seek in a faith community. In these ways, the practice of a signing bonus re-forms the inherited congregation in its relationship to the broader church in faithful and helpful ways.

How then does this practice form the new leader and the new faith community for the broader church? Two key areas of formation here are gratitude and partnership. Love cannot be bought, but there is a difference between money meant to bribe and money meant to support someone's holistic thriving. Particularly for millennials, the generation entering ministry as a first career currently, financial support does not generally mean luxury, it means financial sustenance and the acknowledgment of economic realities this generation faces.[6] A signing bonus of $10,000 is not enough

6. Ivanova, "Millennials Are the Biggest—but Poorest—Generation."

to permanently change someone's lifestyle from Motel 6 to the St. Regis, and it is not enough to financially vindicate a choice for ministry over a job in finance, or even a choice for church planting over a job in an inherited community. It is enough to say, "We believe in you and we are investing in you. We want to support your transition into this position, and your ability to live locally. We want to mark with generosity the promise that we are in this with you." This kind of support on the front end creates a gratitude that pays dividends in trust. You do not offer a signing bonus to someone you do not both trust to stay in the work and believe will do it well. Here the money is practically helpful and, because money is our culture's chosen symbol for value, the planter receiving this gift is invited to recognize the value they bring to the broader church that invites them to this work. The signing bonus serves as a picture of the broader church's very real stake in their thriving. This does not guarantee gratitude leading to trust (nothing does), but the vulnerability and generosity shown by the church offers an essential condition for the thriving of such gratitude and trust.

The second area of formation, partnership, is related to, but distinct from, gratitude. One of the issues mentioned above in the "pastor as hired professional" paradigm, is that the pastor is meant to do the programmatic work of the church that he alone is expert in. This model does not provide much space for partnership because of the natural division in roles that the economic metaphor offers. If the pastor is the CEO and the congregants are the shareholders, he works for them, and ultimately, he, not they, are responsible for the growth that benefits them. The metaphor structure does not allow for the partnership that is necessary for ministry. A signing bonus, particularly in a more moderate size, shifts this. It begins the conversation immediately outside the idea of production in exchange for money. The most important piece of this first transaction is to recognize the human needs of the leader and support them before that leader even begins to produce. Starting on a human level opens a conversation and even negotiation about whole life issues and needs. This funding is meant to enable the new leader to thrive—what else might help them to thrive?

What might help the gathering community to thrive? How might thriving open new possibilities for listening, seeing, and sharing stories of the Holy Spirit's movement in the community? If the leader's role in the community is governed by the exigencies of efficiency and economics, they are less likely to make or claim space for the sorts of connections that can sustain the sharing of the faith. To put it more concretely, for example, if the new leader is calling a caterer, making copies, finalizing a lease on a space, and taking attendance, it is harder for that leader to look up from their busy work to connect with the person across from them at the coffee shop in a meaningful way. And, because of the economic norms of our culture, if the pastoral leader is not doing that kind of connecting work—claiming space for it and both living and proclaiming it, it is not likely that others will initiate conversations beyond the transactional in and beyond the faith community either. Indeed, part of the work of the pastoral leader is to be human and invite others into conversations on that level, so that all might have space to consider the thriving God has for us. Being human cannot be summed up or accomplished through tasks, however specialized. The signing bonus offers space for the leader to be a full and human partner, with both gifts and needs concretely acknowledged even before they begin the work.

The signing bonus also sets the broader church up as partner, not only to the pastoral leader, but to the community where they are planting. Both the leader and, as they articulate it, the broader community, will know that their shared life is a gift made possible by the broader church. Vulnerable neighborhoods particularly understand that nothing is for free and have grown accustomed to having religious leaders who are production arms of other faith communities, rather than gifts of presence who are responsive to their local gifts and needs, sent without agenda from the broader church. Only the latter is free to be a full partner, both to the community and the broader church. If funding and finances are tied to production goals set by an outside body, then the local community is not a partner, they are an object. The signing bonus shifts the metaphor instead to an investment in the potential of both a leader and a community from the start, before anything has been produced. That $10,000 articulates symbolic and concrete value to the leader and community.

Now to the value of $10,000. Since we started this book project, the PC(USA) Board of Pensions has begun to offer a program called Healthy Pastors, Healthy Congregations that "brings a pastor and congregational leadership together to work toward financial sustainability by providing financial education and consultations to both the pastor and congregational leaders."[7] A key provision of this program is that upon completion of the program, the pastor receives $10,000 toward either debt or a retirement savings account. While they don't explore how the board arrived at a $10,000 figure, it seems their goals—for partnership between pastor and congregation and for financial thriving and faithfulness[8]—run parallel to the goals of offering a signing bonus. My own reasoning for this figure relies on my own experience. Early on in my planting ministry, I was awarded a fellowship that included a $10,000 stipend for my personal use. At the time, I was living just outside my immediate parish, in an apartment that I managed to land because the landlord allowed me to move in mid-month, so that first month's rent, last month's rent, and security deposit became half of first month, then last month, and security deposit. I was newly married to a seminary student and living month-to-month; we sold my ancient car because the insurance was too onerous. In that season, the $10,000 became a down payment on our first home, in the community I served, in a major American city, with the help of a mortgage program that allowed us to put less than 5 percent down and offset much of the transfer taxes. That $10,000 was just enough to afford me the stability to serve that community sustainably while building a foundation for a life in ministry. As a result, that $10,000 has been the deciding difference in multiple life-changing decisions since that time—moving, buying another home, saving for retirement, being present in the community I have been called to serve. Since I was awarded that stipend five years ago, I have without hardship,

7. PC(USA), "Healthy Pastors, Healthy Congregations."

8. PC(USA), "Healthy Pastors, Healthy Congregations."

given well more than that amount back to the faith community I started. The number is not perfect for every context, nor is it magic, but it is often substantial enough to change things significantly, while moderate enough to be implemented in a variety of contexts. Additionally, a signing bonus enables the money to be used for something larger—a home, a more reliable car, a significant student loan payment—eliminating or reducing reliance on smaller monthly payments. The difference between that kind of investment and the doling out of the same money over five years is significant, both concretely and symbolically as we explored above. Both the amount and the way the sum is given matters.

With all this in mind, we return to our original goal—could something like this, a signing bonus for planters of new faith communities, particularly in the PC(USA), disrupt "the heresy that" *our congregation* "is the only safe and sanctioned place where the honesty, safety, and joy of being" *spiritual* "creatures may be touched and celebrated"? Could a shift like this invite us to see our citizenship not in our congregation, but rather as part of the entire church ecosystem? Could this practice help us reimagine our economic metaphors for life in the church and expand our understanding of partnership as something we owe our pastors, the broader church ecosystem, and even the world we are called to live in? Could concretely acknowledging the human needs and situations of our pastors, the incalculable value of our communities, and the ultimate allegiance we owe to the church, rather than our congregation, really be accomplished in this small signing bonus? Perhaps it cannot be entirely accomplished there, but I wonder if we might begin to see things anew in such a shift of practice. Within the church ecosystem, new faith communities are often sites of great imagining and re-visioning. Perhaps a signing bonus might be a place where leaders and members of inherited churches might partner with new faith communities in this work, so that we might better share in what the Holy Spirit is doing, rather than holding back gifts we have been given in a way that idolizes our own congregations—because, as we have seen in the book of Acts, that is dangerous practice.

3

Sustainability in God's Good Order

Barry Ensign-George

Introduction

A movement of new, innovative church communities and a centuries-old denomination would seem to mix like oil and water. And yet. Over nearly ten years, the 1001 NWC movement in the PC(USA) has inspired and supported the launching of hundreds of new communities of people living out faith in Jesus Christ together. These communities have been church for many who had not been part of the church, reaching beyond those already in the PC(USA). The movement and the communities that have grown in and through it have been marked by vision and creativity, by heart and passion.[1]

The NWC movement and the communities[2] established by the program have done so within a denomination that traces its direct roots back more than three centuries. It is not an obvious place for such a movement. The PC(USA) has sustained a recognizably common life for more than three centuries across deep

1. PC(USA), "1001 New Worshipping Communities."

2. Hereon NWC refers to both the programmatic movement and the communities that were formed out of its efforts, unless otherwise stated.

changes that have come sometimes suddenly and sometimes very gradually. It is a denomination characterized by internal organization (polity) intensely concerned for an orderliness that would (ideally) enable its members to live and work together in ways that build flourishing—both for those who are part of it, and for the people and communities it touches. One of its common phrases is "decently and in order." Across its long life, the PC(USA) has developed often elaborate institutional structures and systems. In and through these structures, it lives out the Christian faith in distinctive ways.

Yet the denomination is the place where the NWC is rooted. It has provided space for the NWC, a space in which the denomination's drive for order is checked by the drive of the gospel of Jesus Christ to reach out with good news for all. The denomination has provided resources for these new communities—coaching for leadership, conferences for training and networking, cohort groups, staff support, expertise in best practices, wisdom—to come into being, to take shape, to establish a life together that will last.

Rooted in the denomination, the NWC movement has brought into the denomination its creativity and innovation, and the knowledge that yes, Presbyterians can innovate, can work in ways other than "the way we've always done it." Not only the knowledge, but the reality of innovation itself. New worshipping communities require that the denomination think and rethink its understanding of what it is to be a congregation, what is required for worship to proclaim the gospel of Jesus Christ, what it is to be a member, what we are capable of doing here and now, what resources are needed for faithful ministry, and on and on. In grappling with these questions, the denomination renews its faith, its understanding of God's mission in the world, and how we live it.

New worshipping communities and the denomination each bring to the other something needed. Together they embody the basic human truth, "I need you."

As new worshipping communities take shape and continue through time they face, eventually, a new challenge: the challenge of sustainability. Resources dedicated to helping new worshipping communities start and establish a life together no longer fit when they begin to move well beyond the getting-established stage. Sustaining community life is a different task from launching it. Moving through the shift from starting to sustaining requires an understanding of sustainability—what it is, what it requires, what decisions need to be made in order to make that shift well—so that the community's ministry can thrive. Sustaining new worshipping communities is vital both for the NWC and the denomination.

I watch the NWC movement and the communities it has launched with curiosity, interest, amazement, and gratitude. But I am not an insider. I served as pastor of two yoked congregations that have passed the century mark. This was followed by ministry as a staff member of the PC(USA). What does one whose ministry is in an institution carrying centuries of reinforced structures have to contribute to a conversation about new, outside-the-box, nimble, low-structure communities of Christ followers (who is in many ways the embodiment of commitment to low-structure communities)? What I can offer is some reflection on sustaining a collective project across time. What follows is a brief reflection on God's gift of human capacity to organize in ways that call forth and coordinate the gifts and efforts of many in pursuit of shared commitments over an extended period of time. It is an effort to think about how institutional structures sustain a shared effort across many people over time.

The first thing to consider is sustainability, which means thinking about time, and about what lasts a long time, what lasts a short time, and what lasts somewhere in between. The next thing to think about is what forms or structures enable a human endeavor to last over time. Specifically, this means thinking well about institutions. Institutions are about sustaining a human project across space and time (in particular, the project of being a community faithfully following the way of Jesus Christ). They are about sustaining a project on the basis of something that reaches further than personal relationships can carry us. Sustaining new worshipping communities will mean adopting and adapting institutional elements into the lives of these communities. Those who have understood themselves and their worshipping communities as critical of or opposed to "institutional religion" will, I hope, find what follows to be an opportunity to explore what it is that they are rejecting, in order to discover what not to reject. Finally, I will reflect on the relationship between the denomination and the NWC.

Sustaining: Keeping Something Alive over Time

Sustainability is the ability to keep something alive through time. Institutional structures and procedures are means by which humans sustain initiatives that involve the efforts of many people, and that endure over long periods of time. As such, institutions are among God's gifts to human creatures. The anti-institutionalism that has been a primary element of American culture fails to see this reality.[3]

Things vary in their ability to remain alive over time. Sequoia trees live over a very long period of time, however, a dogwood's blossom lives only a short time. Sustaining the blossom is a very different project from sustaining the tree.

Movements generally include elements, often their most exciting elements, that cannot last over time. The excitement surrounding a vision of something new and different, the energy and focus that are called forth by the first stages of work on something new—overcoming challenges, working through the realities that begin to teach it what it is—this excitement, energy, and focus cannot be sustained indefinitely. The personal relationships forged in carrying out a shared vision, often in challenging circumstances, cannot continue at high intensity as time stretches long. Life happens. We change, finding new opportunities and challenges that draw us away from things in which we have been invested. If our shared work is to continue it will have to continue in a different form.

Keeping things alive over time may require significant change of context, thereby changing the thing itself. A dogwood blossom can be preserved, in part, and only by changing it. The blossom

3. Help in thinking well about institutions can be found in Heclo, *On Thinking Institutionally*.

lives for an all-too-brief time but it can be preserved if dried and pressed. Dried and pressed, the blossom continues on, recognizable as a dogwood blossom, but existing in a very different form. Something similar happens in our culture with works of religious art. Paintings created to be part of an altar are kept alive by being placed in museums. This is a profoundly different context, which affects the way they function. But it does not erase their religious function. A friend once commented on being with an ecumenical group that visited a museum whose collection included icons. Group members in the Orthodox tradition engaged the icons not as art works but as icons, religious objects. The icons' religious meaning and function survived their placement in a context shaped by and for different ends. New worshipping communities making the shift to sustaining what has started will work through such questions: What can be sustained? In what form?

Sustaining and Discernment

Movements take institutional form so that some key elements of the movement can live on beyond the necessary excitement, energy, and focus that are crucial parts of its first steps. Identifying the movement's key elements requires discernment, identifying what is to be sustained, and what is of the moment and should be let go. Discernment may conclude that the movement had a limited or short-term lifespan, or that specific forms the movement has taken have run their course. A new worshipping community may in fact discern that it was of a particular moment.

Discernment is not necessarily a value judgment. What is of the moment is as much to be celebrated as what is sustained. The reverse is true as well: what is to be sustained is as much to be celebrated as what is of the moment. The saying "fail fast" points to the potential value of that which is of the moment. That saying suggests a similar saying that would make the same point: "succeed fast, and move on." Some things that do not, or even should not, be sustained are nevertheless important in clarifying possibilities and opportunities.

What is experienced in a new worshipping community can survive. New worshipping communities will survive most strongly in the members of the community, who carry with them the community's impact on their lives. Beyond individuals, another institutional structure will need to be established to sustain what has been learned for the benefit of other communities. For the NWC movement this institutional responsibility belongs to mid-councils and the denomination as a whole.[4] The NWC movement does not exist outside the denomination but is part of it. For those in the PC(USA) who are not part of the NWC movement, the movement is not "them." It is us. Stewardship of the NWC is the responsibility of presbyteries and the denomination broadly, including the responsibility to preserve and share what is being learned.

A final note on discernment. We are likely to differ in our discernment of what is to be sustained and what can be let go. "Differ" is a round-about way of allowing room for disagreement and conflict in this process. We should not be surprised to find ourselves in the midst of conflict over our differing discernments. The challenge we face is to disagree in such a way that our disagreements are not an end point, but a catalyst to insight.

Institutions: Interdependence

If institutions are means by which we sustain initiatives over time, how do we think well about them?

Institutions exist because we are creatures, not God, and are thus finite and interdependent.[5] Like all creatures we are finite—limited in time and space, skills and abilities. This means that we are dependent on others who are not present when and where we are, who have the skills and abilities we need but lack. It

4. "Mid-councils" in the PC(USA) refers to presbyteries and synod. Presbyteries are the key mid-councils for new worshipping communities.

5. My thinking about these matters has been shaped by reflection on and writing about a theological understanding of denomination. Some of that reflection can be found in my "Denomination as Ecclesiological Category," 1–21. I explore it at greater length in *Between Congregation and Church*.

is a basic affirmation of the Reformed tradition, held in particular by the Presbyterian tradition: God alone is able to be fully self-sufficient, creating creatures not out of need but out of divine love. People, like all creatures, are finite and irreducibly interdependent. Nothing we do is fully self-sufficient. We often live out of need.

Interdependence comes in healthy and unhealthy forms. Healthy interdependence involves both dependence and dependability. It enables us to acknowledge that we are dependent on others, some of whom are known to us and some of whom are not. Healthy interdependence means that just as we are dependent on others, others are dependent on us. Healthy interdependence also offers us specific ways to appropriately be dependable for others. Healthy sustainability requires both: deep acknowledgment of our dependence on others, deep embrace of our own dependability. When functioning well, institutions are ways of living healthy interdependence. Unhealthy interdependence tips the balance between dependence and dependability. Institutions that carry unhealthy forms of interdependence are institutions that are not functioning well (there will be more said about this, if briefly, below).

Institutions: Coordination, Perdurance, and Preservation

Institutions coordinate the efforts of a large number of people, enabling them to work together to live out their shared commitment to a long-term project. Institutions enable us to do things we cannot do on our own, or as a small group. They do so by providing ways for us to relate to one another without having to negotiate those relationships one by one on our own. This coordination happens both in the present (synchronously) and through time (diachronously).

In the present (synchronously), institutions coordinate the efforts of a large number of people presently living. Often these people will be spread apart geographically. Almost always this includes people who do not know one another. An institution enables people to be part of a shared project even if they are not able to establish a personal relationship with one another. The

PC(USA) is an example. The denomination brings people who do not personally know one another into relationship by enabling them to be part of a shared commitment to living out faith in Jesus Christ in the ways distinctive to this denomination.

The experimentation being carried out by the NWC is part of a common effort that includes not-new worshipping communities. Worshiping communities new and not-new are joined in living out the Christian faith in distinctively Presbyterian ways. As an institution, the denomination coordinates the different ways in which we do so, making us part of a shared, common project. This coordination helps provide ground on which the two kinds of worshipping communities can share with and in one another. We can do so because we are, in a meaningful way, engaged in a common work.

Over time (diachronously), institutions make it possible for people living at different times to join in a common project. Institutions bring us into relationship with people no longer living and with people not yet born. Coordinating present with past and future institutions enables something to endure across time.

The experimentation being carried out by the NWC is part of a common effort that includes people who went before us. This coordination over the long stretch of time can help those engaged in innovative work see clearly the difference between innovation and creation *ex nihilo*. Innovation—for example, the innovation being carried out in the NWC—builds on existing insights, affirmations, and structures.

Awareness of our connection to those who went before can help existing congregations see that innovative efforts are growing in the same soil in which they were established. We become aware that new worshipping communities are embodiments of the same deep commitments and impulses at work in existing congregations—put otherwise, they are embodiments of the same faith in Jesus Christ that not-new worshipping communities seek faithfully to embody. Here again this awareness can help new communities and not-new congregations see one another as "us", rather than "them."

There is another point to consider. Institutions are able to do their coordinating work because they rely on internal financial resources. Existing congregations are funded primarily by some combination of giving by present members and what has been bequeathed to them by those who have gone before. The same is true for the denomination and its various councils. This is a key issue for new worshipping communities as they move from starting to sustaining.

Institutions Gone Wrong

We know that some institutions do not work in these good ways. It is important to know this, to be articulate about this as well. Being articulate about ways institutions go wrong can help us have language for situations that result in harm.

First, and above all, institutions have regularly been used to oppress. They have been set up or modified to coordinate people in patterns of oppression spread across space and through time, without requiring personal relationship—relationship that would have the power to confront those who benefit from oppression with the harm inherent in those benefits. There have been institutions structured to silence voices that are unwelcome, particularly voices that are perceived to threaten what those in power believe needs—or simply what they want—to be preserved.

Second, even institutions established and sustained for good and faithful reasons are susceptible to going wrong in ways inherent to what they are. These problems arise when an institution loses sight of the project that it was established to carry forward. Institutions can become committed to keeping a project alive that is no longer needed. Instead of being the means to an end (a project), institutions can become committed to preserving themselves, becoming an end in themselves. One of the great contributions of the NWC movement is its power to remind the denomination of the multifold mission to which it is committed.

Denomination (Institution) and the NWC (Experiments, Less Structured Embodiments)

In the best-case scenario, a power grid is in place to link the NWC movement, existing congregations, and the mid-councils of the PC(USA)—a place for continued growth of all three. The grid would be rooted in a "this is all of us" mentality, not us versus them.

Congregations that have sprung up from the NWC movement exist in a polity space that has been shaped with the intention that they have as little predetermined structure as is necessary. At the same time, it is not a space with no structure, and the structure it has is deeply rooted in the Presbyterian ways of living out faith in Jesus Christ. The aim is to create a space that nurtures experimentation and innovation. Determining the minimal necessary structure requires an ongoing reexamination of existing structures, to sort out what is necessary for what kinds of worshipping communities and contexts. This reexamination has been happening since the start of the NWC, is underway now, and will continue.

Reflection on necessary structures needs to consider time frames: some things can function healthily with minimal structure for a short period of time but are unable to remain healthy in that minimal structure over a long period of time. Determining the minimal necessary structure also requires clarity about the central commitments and values that necessitate the structures. Clarity about commitments and values increases our ability to see what is necessary, for what purposes.

I Need You

Central to the sustainability of the NWC movement is the ability to acknowledge that I need you. This is basic to our being as creatures of Creator God. We are inescapably finite, irreducibly interdependent. To say "I need you" is a simple statement of fact. But it need not only be a statement of fact. It might also be a way of asking for relationship that is personal, alert, and attentive. It might be a statement of love and the need to be loved.

The PC(USA) was wise and right to open within itself space for the NWC movement to come into being. Existing congregations and councils of the denomination need the NWC, for reasons I've tried to make clear. The NWC movement needs existing congregations and councils for reasons that I hope are clear. Now the NWC, along with existing congregations and councils, faces the challenge of discerning how new worshipping communities that are well established, that are committed to living on through and beyond the shift from starting to sustaining, are to make that sustaining happen. The same challenge faces the denomination and the NWC itself. The details of how that sustaining happens are going to be worked out in a case-by-case way. If it is worked out it will be an expression of the basic truth, I need you.

4

Stewards of Grace

New Worshipping Communities in a Consumerist Age

Scott J. Hagley

Several years ago, the Target Corporation began an advertising campaign using the phrase "Expect More, Pay Less." Featuring primary colors and a sparse aesthetic, the campaign promised an oasis for world-weary consumers: shopping at Target is bound to improve one's situation with minimal cost. It may not be great advertising, but it is a pithy encapsulation of consumer practice. To be alive in the postindustrial West is to engage the world as consumers, to live within the rules and reasons of the market economy. We take as common sense the accumulation of goods through transactions made in self-interest. In short, we buy low and sell high; we expect more and pay less. This largely works. While we enjoy the fruits of well-functioning and efficient markets for goods and services—the efficiency of an Amazon Prime purchase or the convenience of social activism at the cash register ("Do you want to contribute $1 today to support the SPCA?")—we do not always reflect upon the consequences of putting everything up for sale: breathing air purified for us by Whirlpool and drinking water sponsored by Coca-Cola while enjoying leisure activities monitored by Garmin and uploaded to Facebook.

In what follows, I explore ways in which the "expect more, pay less" rationality of consumer transaction subverts the stewardship practice and theology of new worshipping communities. Because particular tensions remain unresolved in our understanding of stewardship, our vision for sustainable new congregations implicitly accepts the acquisitive, autonomous, and competitive dimensions of economic practice. But new church development can challenge prevailing assumptions regarding stewardship and what constitutes sustainability. Rather than mirror our consumerist age, emerging and fiscally vulnerable new congregations evoke an alternative economic imagination, where we mark sustainability in relationship to our vocation as "stewards of the manifold grace of God" (1 Pet 4:10).

Stewarding the Consumerist Status Quo

The term "stewardship" conjures images of sustainability, tithing, penny-pinching, committees and, perhaps, institutional preservation. In many congregations, it carries a conservative cast: bespectacled, brooding eyes poring over Excel spreadsheets, nervously tapping a pencil on the desk while running calculations to preserve the status quo and keep the organization in operation. Of course, such images trade in unfair stereotypes. Stewardship theology and practice invites us to live faithfully in light of God's abundant generosity. In some frameworks, "steward" lays claim to a whole theological anthropology, recognizing our shared human vocation as one of partnering with God in the care of God's creation.[1] Yet, because the currents of consumer transaction are so powerful, the stereotypes of stewardship are not far from the mark. In the context of a market economy, invitations to stewardship effectively steward the consumerist status quo.

1. This is best represented in the work of Douglas John Hall, who sees far-reaching implications for the symbol "steward" in thinking about biblical theology and the broad structures of the human vocation. See Hall, *Steward.*

Markets provide an efficient and rational means for distributing goods and services by bringing self-interested economic agents together. In basic economic theory, markets work by finding a price point that balances supply and demand. Rational actors collaborate in creating processes by which services and goods are priced and distributed to maximize value for both seller and consumer. In theory, efficiencies are found as all participants expect more (goods, services, profit, etc.) while hoping to pay less.[2]

In recent decades, enthusiastic cheerleaders for market efficiencies have gone in search of new goods to trade, resulting in market processes and rationalities shaping more and more elements of modern life. In *What Money Can't Buy*, Michael Sandel finds countless examples, such as placing advertising on people's faces, paying children to read in troubled school districts, and paying people to wait in line for free Broadway tickets, to name a few. In each of these cases, the "logic of buying and selling," what Sandel calls "market rationality" distributes various social goods not previously considered for sale.[3] Sandel raises two objections to our present market saturation: inequality and corruption. The reasoning follows that if education, air, and water become subject to market forces, then these basic elements of life become more available to those with means. Because markets only make sense in a context of scarcity, reliance upon market forces to distribute goods results in unequal access to the goods for sale. Those with more money can purchase more of the product, increasing its scarcity and/or driving up the price for others. For this reason, markets are not morally neutral mechanisms for distributing goods and

2. Of course, this is an abstract account of how markets actually work. In reality, markets are created and subject to a range of economic, political, environmental, and cultural factors. There isn't, in the end, a single "invisible hand" guiding "the market" toward efficiency, but rather a host of actors and impersonal forces within which buying and selling takes place. By talking about "market rationality," I want to focus on the human and habitual elements of present economic practice. Market ideologies aside, how does our participation in the consumerist economy shape our relationships with one another and God? See, for example, Gay, *Cash Values*.

3. Sandel, *What Money Can't Buy*, 6.

capital.[4] They have an effect on the good being traded, situating it within a context of scarcity and treating it like a commodity. While many things necessary for human life can be exchanged through markets, some things become corrupted when subject to market rationality; some things, like education or religion, fundamentally change when commodified.

Within this context, it is almost impossible to talk about stewardship without theological engagement with market rationality. And yet, this is what we attempt to do. Standard approaches to stewardship begin with God's dominion over all creation and move toward human management of the created and economic order.[5] The metaphor "steward" implies managerial service, and yet our acquisitive context evokes a concern for our own possessions. We see in God's dominion over all creation a mirror for the rational management of our own goods, money, and abilities. Stewardship rarely interrogates the means by which we have acquired our possessions, our attachment to autonomous consumer choice, the broad systemic costs of economic competition, or even our theology of possessions. It largely assumes these elements of the current economic order and seeks to help people of faith to be wise and just managers of their accumulated wealth.[6]

4. This is a key part of Sandel's argument. The way in which a good is exchanged shapes the good itself.

5. Douglas John Hall, who has written extensively about stewardship, follows this logic. The human being exercises stewardship in relationship to God's dominion over all creation. In the first part of *The Steward*, he traces the breadth of biblical meaning for the term, drawing out its managerial content before extending it into a broad symbol for the human vocation. While Hall provides significant depth to this way of approaching stewardship, his argument is fairly traditional. Christians in the United States have all heard fundraising appeals that begin with God's dominion over the earth and then suggest that we give generously from the goods we presently own. This is a long-standing tradition in American Christianity that can date back to the early years of mission on the "frontier." See Walls, *Missionary Movement*, 221–40. For this reading of Hall, I'm helped by Johnson, *Fear of Beggars*.

6. Popularly, we can talk about stewarding our "time, talent, and treasure." Or, in programs like Dave Ramsey's "Financial Peace University," which equates stewardship with wise management of money. Ramsey encourages fast payment of all debt, and then living off of 80 percent of one's income, giving

Because of this ambiguity, calls for stewardship rarely imagine an alternative to our consumerist, market-saturated context. In fact, one cannot properly exercise stewardship without achieving some level of independence and rational control over resources. Fundraising drives compete with one another to wrest both dollars and time or talent away from rational agents stewarding them. Stewardship classes in our congregations help members to understand market mechanisms for wise money management and the distribution of generous financial gifts. Such classes equip members for financial agency and also self-sufficiency, enshrining middle-class norms for life and consumption.[7]

New worshipping communities are shaped in particular ways by this lack of theological engagement with market rationality. Because our framework for stewardship assumes the competitive accumulation of goods, we create perverse incentives for the cultivation of new communities and discipleship practices. In short, the political and economic witness of new communities risks being muted by sustainability and stewardship discourse. Two particular concerns arise at this point. First, church planting remains tethered to market values, such as competition, scarcity, and self-sustaining independence. Second, because we desire self-sufficiency, we rarely expect new worshipping communities to offer alternative economic and political spaces.

Market rationality operates on a principle of scarcity, where limited production creates value. As mentioned above, this rationality governs increasingly diverse elements of modern life. Even our religious life, structured by the congregation as a voluntary association, has been described by sociologists of religion as a "religious economy."[8] The American religious story can thus be told with clear winners and losers based on financial and numerical metrics.[9] Such frameworks are implied when we in the PC(USA)

a 10 percent tithe to a local church and investing 10 percent in savings. See Ramsey, "Financial Peace University," https://www.daveramsey.com/fpu.

7. See again Ramsey, "Financial Peace University."

8. See Finke and Stark, *Churching of America*.

9. The religious economy described by Finke and Stark traces "winners and

make a case for church planting as a response to precipitous numerical decline. We are, without a doubt, losing market share and faced with real questions of scarcity and value. We close once-thriving church buildings and consolidate others. But like a cartoon character trying to plug holes in a leaky dam, these efforts offer us little reprieve. 1001 New Worshipping Communities promises reinforcements for those plugging the dam. Equipped with money, entrepreneurial energy, and several years of unmitigated success, the movement appears healthy. Yet, we rarely call into question the basic market rationality we use to narrate the decline of the church. And this means that our metrics of scarcity infuse our planning for sustainable, successful experiments in cultivating new communities.

By failing to narrate our present situation in non-market terms, we have unwittingly created a situation where the rural and postindustrial spaces of "fly-over" country are both forgotten and under-resourced. Reflecting the logic of scarcity and assuming middle-class images of sustainability and economic efficacy, we strategize new communities in places that reflect some kind of competitive advantage. Markets distribute goods efficiently, but not fairly. There are no good reasons, from the standpoint of long-term market growth or sustainability, to focus energies on spaces scarred by poverty and searching for a future.[10] In a time of relative scarcity, we reason it best to cut our losses. Practiced in stewarding the status quo, we are often ill-equipped to imagine our shared work on different terms.

---

losers" based on financial and numerical metrics. For example, they narrate the success of the Methodists in the nineteenth century against the relative failure of the Congregationalists. The Methodists, they suggest, recognized a religiously competitive context and innovated with ministries and organization throughout the nineteenth century. Congregationalists and others remained static and conciliatory with each other, losing a competitive advantage.

10. I am not suggesting that there are no good reasons for new church development in these places. I am suggesting that the competitive logics we employ can lead us to think that, for these are not communities that tend to draw entrepreneurial talent, nor are they likely to support self-sustaining congregations or substantially add to the head count of the PC(USA).

Thus, we expect new worshipping communities to achieve some level of self-sufficiency, where enough funds can be raised from the community to support the work of ministry. In this way, new worshipping communities actively promote the ambiguous nature of stewardship theology, encouraging the accumulation of goods to provide income for the community. New worshipping communities may intend a provocative engagement with consumerist assumptions, but strong currents of market rationality subvert and submerge such intentions. Whatever the community intends with respect to its political or economic witness, its very existence depends upon and reflects market forces.

Stewarding a Renewed Economic Imagination

In every major American city, people sit at busy intersections with an open hand as a witness to the capricious efficiencies of our consumerist economy. Most of us, most of the time, walk right by them without making eye contact. We see begging as an economic anomaly, a condition that raises suspicion instead of pity or compassion. This was not always so. In *Fear of Beggars*, Kelly S. Johnson recalls the role begging played in the medieval church to provide an alternative economic imagination.[11] A host of medieval saints lived completely dependent upon the gifts of a community. Such vulnerability was seen as a gift to the broader community. The saintly beggar blesses the community, and the community gives the beggar what she or he needs to survive. Such an arrangement witnesses to an economy of grace, providing a window into human interdependence and our naked vulnerability before God. In a time when the early habits of modern economics began to take hold—the monetization of goods and services alongside property rights and modern bookkeeping—beggars offered a different economic vision: gift over transaction, interdependence rather than autonomy.[12]

11. See Johnson, *Fear of Beggars.*

12. Johnson suggests that the ministry of St. Francis of Assisi was particularly powerful in this regard. Johnson, *Fear of Beggars*, 51–69.

New worshipping communities are not exactly beggars, but the risky work of cultivating new community with limited finances and few congregational structures provides the possibility of a different economic, not only ecclesial imagination. To do so, however, we need to recover a sense of stewardship that does not assume accumulation, property rights, and self-sufficiency. Rather than frame stewardship in terms of financial accountability, the church needs communities to imagine *themselves* as stewards of God's grace, as participating in the giftedness of God's people. We need to derive our understanding of stewardship from our theology of gift.

Economic ideologies aside, biblical anthropology insists that to be human is to be *gifted*. The human creature receives a world she did not create and in partnership with others under the rule and invitation of Creator God. The "let us make humankind in our own image" of Gen 1:26 and God's invitation to work and till the garden (Gen 2), envisions relationality at the heart of human and divine identity.[13] We are gifted in relationship to God, creation, and human community; in this giftedness, we respond to the relational reality of God.

We reflect this *giftedness* in our ambiguous relationship with possessions and our embodied life as creatures. In one sense, we do not possess anything, as our lives, communities, and world are given to us.[14] And yet, human life is impossible apart from possessions, which both provide for our well-being (clothing, shelter) and serve as a vehicle for self-expression. The Bible calls our inability to rest in this having and not having "idolatry," for as Luke Timothy Johnson says, "every idolatry is a form of possessiveness . . . if we refuse to acknowledge the dependence of our existence on another, then we must work ceaselessly to create ourselves out

13. Social Trinitarians have convincingly argued for understanding *being* in light of *relationality*. As Jean Zizioulas says in reference to Triune being, and by extension human existence: "to be is to be in relation." See Zizioulas, *Being as Communion*.

14. As Luke Timothy Johnson says: "I *am* but do not *have* my own existence. . . . The world itself stands before God as creature, as radically dependent. If the earth is 'his' and we are 'his,' there is not, in the final analysis, a sense in which we truly possess *anything*." See Johnson, *Sharing Possessions*, 52.

of the things around us."[15] The language of *gift* helps us to envision our relationship to possessions as one of freedom and thanksgiving. Gifts, in the end, are meant for circulation and not for possession.[16] In a formal sense, gifts create generalized reciprocity, an economy which obligates us to one another and future others. As creatures, we are free to receive with thanksgiving the gifts of God and community. In freedom we enjoy the various gifts of creaturely existence, and in thanksgiving we recognize them as contingent, fragile, fleeting, and never completely ours.

This anthropology of giftedness invites us to reimagine stewardship in light of our poverty rather than wealth or accumulation.[17] Our lives are not our own, but rather lived within and in response to the grace of God. Born into structures of reciprocity, obligation, and grace, we are contingent creatures. Stewardship is not what we wisely do with what we possess by nature of God's generosity, but rather our witness to giftedness, our participation in a gift economy. In such a framework, we cannot move as easily from God's dominion over all things to our responsibility to wisely steward what possessions we have. Instead, we recognize the relationship between *sharing* our possessions and our fundamental posture of need and vulnerability.

Stewardship, thus understood, offers an entirely different economic imagination from the efficiencies of the consumerist market. We do not envision stewardship as a rational (or even faithful) management of possessions, but rather our participation in God's gift economy. Recognizing the fact that grace does not

15. Johnson, *Sharing Possessions*, 49.

16. For nearly a century, anthropologists have studied the ways in which gift-giving constitutes an economy rather than a singular event. Marcel Mauss's book *The Gift* describes the ways in which ecologies of reciprocity and obligation are created through gift exchange. One key element of his argument is that gifts are in constant circulation, as they bind people and communities to one another. See Mauss, *The Gift*. Philosophers have also picked up Mauss's theories and have entertained prolonged debates about the nature of "the gift" and how to understand reciprocity. See the debate between Derrida and Jean-Luc Marion, for example: Caputo and Scanlon, *God, the Gift, and Postmodernism*.

17. Johnson, *Sharing Possessions*.

circulate like money, we are free to both depend upon others and offer ourselves in return.[18] While money gains value in a competitive context of scarcity, the grace in which we participate is freely and indiscriminately given.[19] As stewards of God's grace, we recognize both our dependence and our wealth, such that stewardship practice participates in the "unconditional giving" of God.[20]

Stewarding the Gift of New Church Development

What does this mean for new worshipping communities? I suggest above that the vulnerability of new worshipping communities invites us to reconsider the ways in which our stewardship paradigms invest us in the economic status quo. Unfortunately, the pervasive and perverse incentives of the market economy subvert attempts to cultivate a new economic imagination in new communities. To conclude this short reflection, I offer a structural and formational implication of the argument presented: new worshipping communities can witness to the grace of God in a competitive economic context by naming and embracing their dependency upon ecclesial systems and networks, while also organizing community life around practices of sharing.

We hope for new worshipping communities to grow into self-sufficient and self-sustaining congregations. In the PC(USA), we have a series of grants that seed new ministries during the developing years until a ministry can figure out long-term funding sources.[21] In a competitive religious economy we assume this to be the natural order of things: raise capital and sufficient market share or else.

18. Kathryn Tanner engages in a formal exploration of grace and money, drawing out significant distinctions between the way both circulate in order to suggest a noncompetitive set of practices for Christian communities. See

19. Tanner, *Economy of Grace*.

20. Tanner, *Economy of Grace*, 63. It is for this reason that Luke Timothy Johnson insists that *sharing possessions* is the mandate and mark of the church. See Johnson, *Sharing Possessions*.

21. In many cases, this funding is extended by partnerships with other congregations, but we intend for ministries to develop a stewardship ministry within the community for long-term financial health.

Besides its ambiguous view of stewardship, this model struggles to imagine vibrant, long-term ministries in places and among people left behind by the last decades of economic growth. Where these ministries do exist, their dependency upon other congregations is understood as benevolence—a small percentage of a congregation's "missions" budget helps the "developing" community.

However, where stewardship witnesses to an economy of grace, we imagine ourselves as necessarily dependent upon, in obligation to, in reciprocal relationships with, the communities, networks, and families to which we belong. The good to which we aspire is not self-sufficiency or competitive advantage, but rather a witness to God's profligate grace. For this reason, we should experiment with structures for supporting new worshipping communities that take congregational interdependence and long-term partnerships as a good toward which we aspire rather than a means to the end of self-sufficiency.[22] It is time we take seriously our language of "mission partners."

Thus freed from the currents of market rationality, new worshipping communities can play a substantial role in reshaping our ecclesial ecology around stewardship. Learning from neighborhood-based movements like Parish Collective and new monastic communities, new worshipping communities should consider ways in which they can organize their possessions, consumer decisions, etc., in a way that witnesses to the economy of grace rather than money. Such a witness is needed for both our churches and our neighbors, that we might be stewards of God's grace in the name and hope of Christ.

22. Elaine Heath and Larry Duggins Jr. talk about the relationship between "anchor congregations" and new monastic and neighborhood missional communities as one way to structure a church ecosystem rooted in gift rather than competition. See Heath and Duggins, *Missional, Monastic, Mainline.*

Section 2

Cultivating Care

Discipleship for New Church Development

5

Sustainable Churches Have Discipled Leaders

Truth-Telling and Truth-Hearing in New and Established Worshiping Communities

Michael Gehrling

In my time running assessments for the PC(USA)'s 1001 NWC movement, I have noticed a group of leaders interested in church planting with some common characteristics. I am referring to a subset of pastors. These pastors have spent a quarter century or more in our Presbyterian system. Most grew up in Presbyterian congregations. Many of them have served the denomination's mid-councils and in national programs. They've attended multiple Presbyterian conferences and have participated in multiple Presbyterian networks or interest groups. They have spent time at most of our seminaries and camp and conference centers. Having spent such a long time so deeply involved in the PC(USA), they are perhaps the most representative "products" of our system.

These veteran Presbyterians have demonstrated a common and troubling characteristic when being assessed as potential new worshipping community leaders: they are often incapable of receiving feedback. Positive feedback bounces off of them. Critical feedback is met with objection or dismissal. When invited to share about formative feedback or counsel they have received from trusted friends or mentors, they're unable or unwilling to do so.

For the vision of 1001 NWC to be realized, the PC(USA) will need to raise up missional, spiritually mature, self-aware leaders to start and sustain them. This essay will argue that disciplines of truth-telling and truth-hearing are vital for leadership in new worshipping communities, and explore how the concept of the priesthood of all believers provides a Reformed theological foundation for such practices.

Let's look first at the formative moments of the first church planters—the apostles. The gospels report Jesus speaking to the Twelve about difficult truths concerning them. Consider Jesus' interactions with Peter. After Peter's failed attempt to walk on water, Jesus says to him, "You of little faith, why did you doubt?"[1]

After Peter's accurate confession that Jesus is the Christ, Jesus says, "Blessed are you, Simon son of Jonah! For flesh and blood has not revealed this to you, but my Father in heaven. And I tell you, you are Peter, and on this rock I will build my church, and the gates of Hades will not prevail against it. I will give you the keys of the kingdom of heaven, and whatever you bind on earth will be bound in heaven, and whatever you loose on earth will be loosed in heaven."[2]

And this affirming feedback is quickly followed by rebuke of Peter's insistence that Jesus not suffer and die at the hands of the religious leaders: "Get behind me, Satan! You are a stumbling block to me; for you are setting your mind not on divine things but on human things."[3]

In Gethsemane, Jesus reflects back to Peter his failure to pray: "So, could you not stay awake with me one hour?"[4]

1. Matt 14:31 NRSV.
2. Matt 16:17–19 NRSV.
3. Matt 16:23 NRSV.
4. Matt 26:40 NRSV.

And in the Upper Room, Jesus reveals to Peter that he is on a path toward denying Jesus: "Will you lay down your life for me? Very truly, I tell you, before the cock crows, you will have denied me three times."[5]

Repeatedly, Jesus holds a proverbial mirror up to Peter, reflecting back to Peter his faithfulness and his sinfulness, his insight and his naiveté. Hearing truth about himself was an essential component of Peter's apostolic journey.

Acts and the New Testament epistles illustrate that this practice of truth-telling and truth-hearing continued in the life of the apostolic church after Pentecost. Paul reports to the church in Galatia that he opposed Peter, pointing out Peter's hypocrisy of eating with, and later separating from, the Gentile believers for fear of his fellow Jews' reaction. In the book of Revelation, John the Seer, having received words from Christ on the aisle of Patmos, sends letters to seven churches offering both affirmation and rebuke.

The continued practice of truth-telling among Christian leaders manifests in the historic church through the practice of spiritual disciplines such as confession, spiritual direction, and spiritual friendship. These disciplines were understood sacramentally. In each, the truth-teller—whether a priest, superior, or spiritual companion—functions as a representative of Christ. Consider the instruction offered by John Climacus in *The Ladder of Divine Ascent*: "At confession you should look and behave like a condemned man. Keep our head bowed and, if you can, shed tears on the feet of your judge and healer, *as though he were Christ*."[6]

The first generations of Christians understood the importance of truth-telling and truth-hearing. The challenging discipleship of Jesus that formed Peter and the other apostles didn't stop after Christ's ascension, but continued through spiritual disciplines in which individual Christians allowed others to represent Christ to them.

This need for truth-telling has also been affirmed by contemporary experts in the area of Christian leadership. Ruth Haley

5. John 13:38 NRSV.

6. Climicus, *Ladder of Divine Ascent*, 108–9.

Barton, cofounder of The Transforming Center and author of multiple books on leadership, describes truth-telling as an essential value for any Christian leadership team:

> We believe that all truth, no matter how delicate or painful or seemingly inconsequential, contributes to the discernment process. God desires truth in the inward being because truth leads to freedom, spiritual transformation, and deeper levels of discernment. Since the Holy Spirit has been given to us to guide us into truth, we seek to offer the truth in love and gentleness rather than hiding truth or "spinning" the truth; anything less than this kind of honesty places the community in great peril.[7]

Of course, truth-telling is pointless without a willingness to hear the truth. It is not a coincidence that Barton also notes that "a willingness to be exposed and vulnerable" is an essential characteristic of anyone "leading toward something that is genuinely new."[8]

In their book *The Ascent of a Leader*, Bill Thrall, Bruce McNicol, and Ken McElrath also speak to these values, and even describe them as prerequisite for any meaningful leadership. The authors describe leadership development in terms of a ladder, each rung representing intentional actions one must take toward gaining meaningful influence and leaving a valuable legacy. The first rung to step onto is to trust oneself to God and others. The second and third are choosing vulnerability, in which the leader deliberately places themselves under the influence of others, and then aligning with truth or choosing to act on the wisdom and truth of that influence.

Barton and the authors of *Ascent of a Leader* describe the commitment to vulnerability, and truth-telling—and hearing, as vital for any leader. For those who would start and lead a new worshipping community, this commitment is absolutely essential.

Unlike established churches where a pastor's personality can be mitigated by years of precedent, established structures and traditions, and congregants whose commitment to the church

7. Barton, *Strengthening the Soul*, 177–78.

8. Barton, *Strengthening the Soul*, 163.

predates the pastor's arrival, new worshipping communities, lacking all of the above, will always reflect the personalities and values of their founders. Leaders who are spiritually and emotionally healthy will start spiritually and emotionally healthy communities. Leaders who are spiritually and emotionally unhealthy will start unhealthy communities. The ongoing health and vitality of their community depends on the leader's willingness to hear others point out her blind spots and to receive their council. When this truth is offered in relationships of grace such as discipleship, spiritual direction, or spiritual friendship, these moments will also provide the experiences of spiritual transformation that will be the fuel for the leader's ongoing motivation.

Without these truth-telling and truth-hearing relationships, the new worshipping community leader will be fueled only by passion or excitement for the project, or professional competencies devoid of spiritual power. The former is finite and puts an expiration date on the community. The latter will at best lead to a sustainable organization lacking transforming discipleship.

For the PC(USA) to fulfill its vision of starting and sustaining 1,001 new worshipping communities, it will need to produce a culture of openness to truth-telling and truth-hearing among its leaders. Doing so will require the recovering and reclaiming of classic spiritual disciplines such as confession and spiritual direction. While some truth-telling disciplines, particularly spiritual direction, have seen a recent resurgence in Protestant circles, we should reflect on the theological foundations of such disciplines, ensuring they are not merely a passing fad.

As already noted above, disciplines of confession and spiritual direction for the ancient church were sacramental acts, in which the confessor or the director provided a tangible experience of Christ's voice. The Protestant Reformation, in its critique of the medieval Catholic division of ordained from laity, and in its emphasis on the priesthood of all believers, should have led to an increase in these disciplines. If all Christians are priests, all are able to represent Christ to others. The Reformed Christian no longer need to rely on the ordained to hear their confession or offer direction. Instead, the Christian should have a whole community of siblings able and willing to provide a sacramental experience of Christ's authority. If the Reformed vision of the priesthood of all believers were realized, every Reformed church (and every new worshipping community) should be a community of priests empowered and willing to represent Christ to their siblings, and simultaneously a community of saints who have received the words of Christ through their siblings.

Instead, Protestant ecclesiology has drifted in the opposite direction, and the spiritual results are not positive. In his work *Spiritual Theology*, Simon Chan offers a particularly pointed critique of the protestant churches' failure to fulfill its vision:

> Historically, when Luther invoked the universal priesthood of all believers and abolished the monastic system, the idea of the church was radically reconceived. Theoretically, it should uplift all believers, but in actual fact it tends to reduce them to the lowest common denominator. We wanted to make everyone in the church into robust saints but succeeded only in making mostly mediocre ones.[9]

When Presbyterians talk about making the priesthood of all believers a reality, we tend to focus on the need to empower all members of the body. Many churches claim as call words, "Every member a minister." Chan, however, suggests that the heart of the problem lies less with unempowered saints and more with a refusal to yield to the authority that comes from that empowerment:

> The Protestant doctrine of the priesthood of all believers has sometimes been distorted into a me-and-my-God egocentrism. We think that because we have direct priestly access to God, we owe obedience to God and no one else. We forget that obedience to God may well come through freely embracing the yoke of human authority. The ancient monks taught us that learning to be under obedience to a human superior is one of the most effective ways of checking our self-will. And

9. Chan, *Spiritual Theology*, 105.

> self-will, not ignorance, is what hinders us from perfect conformity to God's will.[10]

The empowerment of every Christian implicit in the concept of the priesthood of all believers is meaningless if no one yields to the authority that comes from that empowerment. By claiming the priesthood of all believers, we imply that every believer in our churches and new worshipping communities is an intermediary between ourselves and Christ. As such, every member is capable of speaking to any other—including the pastor!—on Christ's behalf.

The priesthood of all believers is a gift from God to be stewarded by every Christian community. The empowerment and authority to represent Christ to others comes not from training or education but from God by the Holy Spirit. The pastor or church planter who faithfully stewards this gift in her community will be the one who is first to recognize that authority in others and yield to it. Rather than being the reason Protestants tend not to practice disciplines of truth-telling and truth-hearing, the priesthood of all believers should be the theological foundation for doing it more frequently than most.

What will this faithful stewardship look like? I offer two suggested practices: spiritual friendship and debriefing.

First, every new worshipping community leader should have a spiritual director and be in a spiritual friendship. By the latter, I mean a long-term, intentional friendship in which each represents Christ to the other. The leader should be open and transparent about these relationships with their community.

Spiritual friendship was the most significant practice that sustained my own ministry as a new worshipping community leader and continues to sustain me today. When I experienced God's call to start a new church, I was fortunate not to receive that call alone, but instead became the organizing co-pastor of our fledgling community. My co-pastor, Chris, and I quickly began a rhythm of meeting weekly strictly for spiritual conversation. The planning and business

10. Chan, *Spiritual Theology*, 150.

of the church was off limits in these conversations. Instead, we structured this conversation by asking one another six questions:

- What is the state of your heart?
- How are you wrestling with "evil heart states"?
- How are you doing loving those closest to you? And how have I been doing loving you?
- How have you heard God speaking in the past week?
- Where have you experienced apostolic success? Where have you experienced apostolic failure?
- How can I pray for you?

These conversations and the times of prayer together that followed became the strength of our shared ministry. Answering these questions led us both to share vulnerably, and to receive the response of the other. In our successes, we gave each other permission to pause for a moment and celebrate. In our shortcomings, these conversations provided moments of grace. Even as God has called us to new and different ministries, and different parts of the country, we continue to have this conversation monthly over the phone.

Second, every leader in new and old forms of church should be debriefing all of the major activities of the community with the whole leadership team.

Though not a biblical word, the concept of debriefing is ubiquitous in the story of Jesus' ministry with the disciples in the gospels. Regularly, Jesus engages in dialogue following his sign acts. After Jesus sends the seventy in Luke 10, they return rejoicing. Then, Jesus offers more teaching and prays with them.

In every church community's debrief, the leader and their team have the opportunity to disciple one another. Debriefing conversations can include questions such as:

- Where did we experience God's work in this activity? For what do we give thanks?
- What did we do well? Where did our talents and spiritual gifts flourish? Where did you see someone else on the team excel?

- What could we have done better? If we were to do this activity again, what should we do differently? Is there anything for which we need to seek forgiveness from God, our neighbor, or one another?
- As we think of our experiences with this activity, what Scriptures come to mind? How might we engage these scriptures in the coming days?
- In light of all of this, what does God have for us next? Are there particular ways we need to learn and grow as a community? Are there particular forms of ministry or service we should pursue?

Such practices demand vulnerability. Practices such as these that involve truth-telling will hold up a mirror to the leaders of our churches and new worshipping communities, causing them to look at aspects of themselves they had previously failed to see or refused to see. They will also provide the moments of spiritual transformation experienced by the Apostle Peter and every other church planter who has founded a community worth sustaining.

6

The Stewardship of Prayer and Play

Aisha Brooks-Lytle

Rejoice always, pray without ceasing,
give thanks in all circumstances;
for this is the will of God in Christ Jesus for you.[1]

Westminster Shorter Catechism—Question 1
Q. 1. What is the chief end of man?
A. Man's chief end is to glorify God, and to enjoy him forever.[2]

Prayer is central to the Christian life. As we continue to live, move, and have our being in God, we are encouraged to connect and commune with God in prayer. Let's be honest: Prayer is a mystery. We can see in the biblical witness and in our own lives that prayer changes situations and circumstances. We can see how prayer changes our perspective. We know that prayer has the power to transform the heart, mind, body, and soul. There are times when it seems natural to pray. There are times when prayer is the last thing we want to do in our ministry and in our daily lives. Yet

1. 1 Thess 5:16–18 NRSV.

2. PC(USA), *Constitution of the Presbyterian Church*, "Westminster Shorter," line 7.001.

I stand as another voice and echo the praying voices of those who came before me and have taught me in the faith. I self-identify as a bridge-builder in the work I have done in a variety of communities—white, black, multicultural, homogenous, rich, poor, urban, and suburban. All of these communities have shaped me and given me language, modes, and methods to navigate through the mystery and matrix of prayer. Thanks to these diverse sacred spaces, I can testify that my life has been changed through my feeble attempts at praying "without ceasing."

Alongside the power of prayer, I also testify to the gift of play. Play is good for the soul. My mother recounts the story of being awakened by my smiling face peering over the crib when I was just a toddler. When the sun came up, I was eager and ready for the fun and adventure a new day would bring. When we were kids, we lived to play with our friends, to run outside, or to play a good board game on a rainy day. Play was central to our existence. Even for those of us who faced difficulty and trauma, play was a reminder that life was meant to be lived with the promise of anticipatory joy, hope, and an active imagination. Play was not an option for me and my friends. It was a prerequisite for learning how to cultivate the art of black girl magic and black boy joy in the face of pain and uncertainty that life can bring. Play was respite and renewal for the soul. Through the gift of play, we found the power of belly laughs and the improvisation of creating silly jokes and participated in the spiritual practice of smiling until our cheeks hurt.

The older we get, the more we seem to rationalize ourselves out of play that is healthy, life giving, and fills our hearts with joy. In the same way that scripture calls us to pray without ceasing, our historical confessions in the Presbyterian church remind us of the importance of enjoyment. The first question of the Westminster Catechism calls us to enjoy all of God and all that God has provided for us.[3] God has created us so that our lives would reflect God's own glory. This call to "enjoy God" continues to capture my attention. What would it look like for leaders to enjoy God in

3. PC(USA), *Constitution of the Presbyterian Church*, "Westminster Shorter," line 7.001.

the gifts of laughter, play, wonder, discovery, and creativity? We live in a world that is fixated on self-serving indulgence. But this catechetical question delivers a twofold answer. Our enjoyment of God is linked to our lives glorifying God. The two go hand in hand. I can think back to my own involvement with the games of my childhood, like double Dutch, hide and seek, dodgeball, riding our bikes, or sitting on the steps listening to our jams on the boom box. We gathered together for a common purpose and collective goodness. We simply enjoyed being together, having fun, and not having a care in the world. For me, the innocence and joy were reflections of God's divine nature of love, beauty, curiosity, energy, and light. We radiated in the sun as we enjoyed the moment and mystery of play. I believe that our childhood play pointed to the beauty of God.

As adults, our play unleashes our ability to see the connection between enjoying God and glorifying God. It appears that we can make sense of the glorifying God, but the enjoyment does not come so easily. It sounds like child's play! Christ himself reminds the disciples that becoming like children is critical for entering the kingdom of God (Matt 10:15). As a child, I remember the power of gathering as many of my friends as possible together to have fun and enjoy one another. We did not care about status or hierarchy. In our playfulness, we were reminded that we mattered, that we needed each other, and playing together fulfilled our unifying purpose of finding joy in the moment. As an adult, becoming like a child has given me the gift of making play a spiritual practice by using my imagination, dreaming for a new world today, and improvising solutions in the face of life's peculiar and difficult moments. For me, play has been, and continues to be, a gift of light that pierces any and every dark place. Play gave me the strength to live as I watched my dying spouse take his final breath at the tender age of forty-three. My late husband's transition from this life to the next was filled with listening to music, laughter, soft smiles, and gentle tears. This gift of learning how to play has become God's gift to me and another means to help me to enjoy God fully and to glorify God day after day.

In the same way that I have found play a lifelong and life-giving practice, prayer has become for me a gift filled with mystery, beauty, patience, and wonder. If we are going to learn to pray without ceasing, then we must get rid of our preconceived notions of prayer. The same imaginative mind that God gives us for play is the same one we can use to imagine God's presence in the sacred moments of prayer. Prayer and play are like partners on the dance floor. They know the same moves. They keep the same rhythm and tempo while moving through variations on the same theme. Watching them in step teaches me how to move through this world with a spirit of openness and gives me a vocabulary of freedom and agility. Through play, God has been cultivating my creativity as an active participant in the holy moments we call prayer.

Only recently have I come to acknowledge that through differing modes and methodologies, I pray more than I realize. When I was younger, I thought that a true prayer warrior was the older woman who got on her knees for hours to call on the name of the Lord. There is no way I could ever pray like that! Yet not long ago, a ministry colleague described me as "a woman of prayer." Here's the truth: I pray all the time. And you probably do, too. I pray when I wake up, while I am driving, when I'm angry, when I'm excited, and when I don't know what to do. I pray when things are going great and I pray when things are a hot mess. In many ways, prayer can be an organic outpouring of our ongoing relationship with God as we seek to lead others and serve the world. I witnessed this mixed methodology of praying in the prayer life of my mother. She talks as openly and freely with me as she does with the God of the universe. She taught me that for every situation there may be a different style or approach to prayer. I believe that prayer can also be practiced in a very intentional way as we make sense of the phases and stages of our ministry and in our lives together.

During my time as the organizing pastor for The Common Place and as the associate pastor for mission at Wayne Presbyterian Church, I noticed that the ministry team used different modes of prayer during the different phases of our new ministry initiative and worshipping community. I counted four modes of prayer used for the diversity of work in our context. I like to think of these four modes of prayer as *strategic*, *sighing*, *spiritual warfare*, and *silence*. Let's start with *strategic prayers*.[4] In the book of James, the epistle writer gives practical wisdom for Christian living. In chapter 5:13–16, we are encouraged to pray when we are suffering, to praise when we are filled with cheer, to call on the elders to pray over us when we are sick, and to confess in our times of frailty and brokenness. The epistle writer declares that the prayers of the righteous are powerful and effective. When we found ourselves planning and visioning, we offered prayers that were detailed and systematic as we trusted God for transformational and effective change. In that way we imaged and trusted a strategic God.

The Common Place came out of a church partnership and became a shared ministry space that provided a safe place to enhance the life of children and their families through faith, education, and social service support. It grew into a safe and sacred space where all the partners involved could "do life together." The concept included a cross-section of ministry partners: an existing African American PC(USA) congregation with building issues, a Christian school who shared a parking lot with that same church, a rich, predominately Caucasian, resourced, suburban PC(USA) congregation with a twenty-year history in this urban community, a Southwest Philadelphia networking group, other partner suburban churches, and our local presbytery. I prayed quietly, "*How, O Lord, will we be able to get the key partners all on the same page so that we can start something new and vibrant in the community?*" We had to use strategic prayers. I have found that in the same ways there are structural and systemic practices that lead to paternalism, division, and control, we need strategic and systematic prayers to break down barriers, to give ministry partners eyes to see the mutuality of gifts, and to ask God to utilize those gifts to rebuild, rejuvenate, and renew.

Anytime you attempt a major culture shift within the PC(USA), there must always be a strategic plan involved. In the case of The Common Place, the leadership at the suburban church

4. Sacks, *Prayer-Saturated Church*, 91.

had a proposal for the session and had conversations with the presbytery. There were handouts and slide shows. But, if you are planning strategically, then along with that, you should also be praying strategically. We had a team of people committed to praying for the people, places, and processes needed to see a spiritual vision become a reality. Strategic prayers need to be saturated in humility and vulnerability. These prayers of detail and order may come easy for the Type A personality or highly organized church culture. With full honesty and humility, every statistic, hope, analysis, and dream needs to be placed at the mercy seat of God so that God's will may be done step by step. I distinctly remember that before the presentation to the session of the suburban congregation, there was a year-and-a-half process of discernment and prayer within the congregation as we considered where God was calling us to invest our time, resources, and spirit.

At the same time, the small African American congregation had been committed to strategic prayers as they envisioned their future. There were key elders and lay leaders who prayed faithfully that God would have a new vision for the ministry on the corner of 58th Street and Kingsessing Avenue. Strategic prayers take into consideration the complexity of the task. Strategic prayers offer specificity and detail back to God and ask God to do the impossible with all the moving parts. Strategic prayers are offered as often as there are scheduled meetings and discussions around the project. Everyone involved in our new ministry was committed to the task of planning for a new adventure and praying for all that was needed to come together. I am convinced that the prayers of the righteous in this process made a way for these partners to come together. A small African American congregation allowed a large Caucasian congregation to purchase its property with the promise to use resources and partnerships to do something beautiful together on that corner. Five years later, with over 1.5 million dollars of investment and too many hands and hearts to count, I am convinced that these strategic prayers have been and will continue to be powerful and effective. These prayers enabled a future of sharing that could not have otherwise been imagined.

In the early days of the building renovations at The Common Place, we all used what I would call *sighing prayers*. In Romans, the Apostle Paul says that in our weakness there is help from the Holy Spirit. Paul reminds us that even though we do not always know how to pray, the Spirit intercedes for us with "sighs too deep for words" (Rom 8:26). This verse was a helpful reminder in our work with The Common Place—that some of our prayers would literally become sacred "sighs" as we looked at each new challenge as something that only God could mend. After both congregations said yes to this new ministry initiative, we had to put together the team of heads, hands, and hearts who could implement the work. When we saw the enormity of the task, there were plenty of sighs.

We walked into the reimagined ministry space knowing that it needed a new roof, new boiler, and interior work completed. We walked into that place knowing that we needed to strengthen the relationship with the original congregation and the partner Christian school. We walked into that place knowing that we had money for building repairs, but we needed funding to start a new after school program and we needed a group to manage it. We walked into the space knowing that we needed to connect with a social service agency that aligned with our core values. We walked in knowing that we wanted to offer a worship experience where children and youth were able to lead and learn to connect with God in a deeper way. We walked into that space knowing that we needed the community to know that we cared and were not simply taking over management of the property. We walked in knowing that we wanted kids to get to know what was happening behind those newly painted bright blue doors. Every time we acknowledged the uncertainty of how we would accomplish the next hurdle, there was a sigh.

Our collective "sighs" created a mosaic of unspoken prayers we offered to God. It was a reminder that with all the gifts among us, we still needed the Spirit's power to articulate the needs and desires of all involved with this ministry adventure. With every sacred sigh, there was a holy reassurance that the Spirit did indeed intercede for us. God heard every sigh, moan, and groan we uttered as we tried to make sense of how to implement the vision.

Sighing prayers hold onto the hope that we may not know how God is going to get us through the next hurdle but we trust that God will do it. In our experience at The Common Place, God met our needs and helped us make sense of the hurdles in ways we could never have dreamed or imagined. Our sighing prayers held the echoes of saints of the past who had dreamed and used their imagination for a ministry that would continue to reach out to children and families from generation to generation and from glory to glory. In our office, we kept pictures of the foundational church leaders from the original ministry that started at The Common Place dating back to the mid- to late 1800s. I knew that their commitment to children's ministry was filled with sighs that were breathed long before I ever took my first breath on this earth back in 1974. The sighs I breathed were not only birthed out of my own observations but contained the spiritual breath of those who had passed the mantle onto the next era of ministerial leadership.

It was out of the sacred and collective sighs of ancestors, community partners, churches, ecumenical supporters, politicians, activists, children, families, leaders, and laity that I realized some of the obstacles in the initial stages of our new and revitalized ministry were a matter of *spiritual warfare*. Yes, I said, spiritual warfare. I did not grow up Pentecostal but I grew up as a Baptist with Pentecostal underpinnings. God has always surrounded me with Pentecostal, tongue-speaking, demon-rebuking Christians. God has always brought those friends in my life at the right time to pray in this way for a particular purpose. In the twenty-plus years that I have served the Lord as a Presbyterian, I have seen the power of intentionally praying against forces of evil, oppression, and negativity. The Apostle Paul speaks to us about this in his letter to the Ephesian Christians. He reminds all who have an ear to hear that "our struggle is not against enemies of blood and flesh, but against rulers, against authorities, against the cosmic powers of this present darkness, against the spiritual forces of evil in heavenly places."[5] On more than one occasion in my ministry, there has been evidence of negative events that have happened in the dark corners of a church property. I read

5. Eph 6:12 NRSV.

through old session minutes and church records that showed a long history of conflict, pain, and dissension. So, I banded together with a group of prayer warriors who prayed for what was obvious but also prayed against unseen forces that have been at work in the history of brokenness in a congregation.

I was afraid to go into the basement of The Common Place. I mentioned to some of my church-planting friends and ministry colleagues that it felt as if "something bad" had happened down there. I had no substantial evidence. I only had confirmation from other members of our faith community that we needed to pray in that space. One of my suburban church members connected with me after worship one week and said, "Aisha, I feel like we are supposed to pray in my basement or in a basement. Does that make sense to you?" *"Crap!"* I thought to myself, *"Now I got other folks talking about that creepy basement."* Instead of shrugging it off, I took seriously the words of wisdom given first to the Ephesian Christians and now to people like us. So, a group of us gathered together in the sanctuary of The Common Place. The prayer was simple. We asked that God would reclaim space in the building that had experienced brokenness and pain. We wanted God's presence to be fully known from the upper room of the building to the basement. We asked God to restore and repurpose that lower level so that it would be a place where children were safe to play and experience God once again.

And then we went as a group into that damn basement. One young man played the guitar and quietly sang praise songs. One clergy woman used anointing oil to make the sign of the cross on the walls. A few women started praying in tongues. Another person was moved to tears. I stood in the middle of the space and declared that anything unclean and not of God was no longer allowed to operate in the space. In that moment of communal prayer, supplication, and a true warrior pose, something shifted in that room. We all felt it. In a spiritual act, we reclaimed the space that had been overshadowed by the darkness of the past. Later, others would share that there were stories of ugliness and pain that had happened in the space. Fast forward to today and that basement is utilized in a way that is healthy, beautiful, and life-giving.

The fourth and final mode of prayer can be described as both the ending and the beginning. I simply call these *prayers of silence*. In the push and pull of a new ministry adventure, you must carve out space to sit somewhere and be still. The truth of Psalm 46:10 speaks volumes to twenty-first-century Christians who are constantly in a state of motion: "*Be still and know that I am God! I am exalted among the nations, I am exalted in the earth.*" There were times when I would slip into the sanctuary of The Common Place when it was empty. There is always something going on in the building, so it is rarely quiet at The Common Place. But even on the busiest of days, I could sit and be still in the presence of God.

In the stillness and in the silence, we have room to breathe with God. In 2018, my ministry colleague, Christian Washington,[6] began and continues to post "breathing pairs" on his social media page. He encourages Christians to take a break in the day to practices spiritual breathing exercises like, "*Inhale*—trust God to—*and exhale*—control." His invitation is a reminder that as we enjoy solitude with God, we can inhale God's grace and mercy and exhale the worries of the day. We can inhale God's joy and peace, and exhale anxiety and frustration. We can inhale awe, and exhale anger and doubt. Being in the presence of God is a deep reminder that God cares more about you than all the work that you do in the name of God. In his book entitled *Emotionally Healthy Leader*, Pete Scazzerro reminds leaders of the importance of finding balance in the rhythm of work and life. He reminds all of us that "who we are is more important than what we do."[7] Breathing and basking in the love and goodness of God reorients us to be still enough to enjoy a moment with God. As a child playing with my friends, I learned that I had to take breaks to catch my breath even if I was having the time of my life. Playing trained me to listen to heart, mind, and soul for the right moment to pause, breathe, and be still

6. Christian Washington, Instagram post, March 17, 2018, http://instagram.com/significancecoach.

7. Scazzero, *Emotionally Healthy Leader*, 38.

before I jumped back into the game. Being still helps us to hit the reset button and to be thankful for everything that has happened and for the gift of being alive to experience it.

As children of God embarking on this new collaborative ministry adventure, we prayed without ceasing and we relearned how to play. In my ministry at The Common Place, play included laughing with my staff. It included taking a break and hanging out with the kids in our after-school program. Play included buying yarn to knit a prayer shawl for a member of the congregation. It meant singing in my car like I was having my own personal karaoke party. It meant taking a walk with friends or having an impromptu dance party in the kitchen. In the middle and muddle of ministry, as you pray, make space to play. Life-giving and soul-stirring forms of play remind us we are called to enjoy God as we glorify God.

As you think about this work, wherever you are in the church ecosystem, this is my prayer for you: I pray that you will be open to the imaginative ways we can communicate with God as we connect with one another. I pray that you will feel free to improvise in your ministry context and collaborate with a host of unlikely ministry partners to do the impossible. I pray that you reject fear and accept the divine invitation to play in the space where God dwells and is engaged in divine creative initiatives. I hope and pray that as you lead and serve in new and creative ways that you create space to have a little talk with God. I hope you infuse your life with play that leads to love, laughter, joy, and delight.

So, I leave you with this image of the intersectionality of prayer and play. As we were in the embryonic stages of forming The Common Place, I had a dream. In this dream, there were three open hands with their palms facing upward. In the palm of each of those hands were Fabergé-like eggs. These ornate eggs were split open, each filled with galaxies and floating planets. I touched one of them and the planets moved as if they were dancing around my fingers. As I woke up from that dream, I heard God say that we had no idea what would come of our work at The Common Place. I will never forget that image or the voice of God whispering in my ear. That experience remains as an open invitation from the God of the universe to play and to pray every step of the way.

7

Learning to Listen

A Relational Approach to Vocation and Discernment

Kristine Stache

As a popular children's story, Moses and the burning bush often finds itself in Bible picture books accompanied by pages filled with bright orange and red flames shooting out from a shrub. Young and old love this story, both for its vivid imagery and the way it kicks off some remarkable events in the next several chapters of Exodus. However, as readers, we are often in such a hurry to get to the drama of Moses' story, the plagues, and the exodus from Egypt that we tend to jump right over what is happening in this important story of call.[1]

Moses' call story, as remarkable as it is, is filled with so many extraordinary elements that we tend to overlook that in many ways, this story is also our story. We, the church, are called in the midst of our ordinary daily tasks to respond to God's invitation to make a difference in the lives of God's people. But we, like most readers, tend to jump over our story of call to get to the tasks at hand. Using

1. Exod 3:1–12 NRSV.

these verses from Exodus as a guide, this chapter hopes to explore God's invitation of call and vocation as gift from God to join God in mission for the sake of the world. How we, as people of God, live out this vocation individually and as life together in the ecologies of our particular places and responsibilities are defined through the stewarding of the many relationships in our lives.

Vocation

> *Moses was keeping the flock of his father-in-law Jethro, the priest of Midian; he led his flock beyond the wilderness, and came to Horeb, the mountain of God. There the angel of the Lord appeared to him in a flame of fire out of a bush; he looked, and the bush was blazing, yet it was not consumed. Then Moses said, "I must turn aside and look at this great sight and see why the bush is not burned up." When the Lord saw that he had turned aside to see, God called to him out of the bush, "Moses, Moses!" And he said, "Here I am."*[2]

What makes these verses so remarkable is the ordinariness in which this story takes place. Moses was out in the wilderness minding his own business tending to his every day, routine work, his father-in-law's sheep. This is where God appeared to Moses. This is where God appears to us. Not just in old, historic churches. Not just on a podium in front of millions, but in the mundane parts of our lives and in the lives of new communities being formed. God's call is not a generic shout-out to whomever happens to be passing by. In these verses God calls Moses by name.

Like the angel in the burning bush, God comes to us and calls us by name. We do not have to do anything, prove anything, or accomplish anything. This is grace. We do not have to have a certain set of skills, abilities, or titles to participate as leaders in the church. God comes to us when we are at our best and at our worst, in

2. Exod 3 :1–4 NRSV.

our broken, inadequate, and lonely lives. God comes to us. This is about what God has done, is doing, and continues to do.

God calls us to join in God's work in the world. Jesus says, "Follow me, and we will figure it out as we go." Over and over God says, "I know you better than you know you. I call you as you are today, not some day in the future when you think you are ready." God assures us that we will figure it out as we go. We learn by trying and failing, not by pretending to be masters. To be a leader is about opening oneself up to transformation, about becoming and being formed. This is countercultural when we are accustomed to aiming for perfection. We get so caught up in thinking we need to do it right, whatever right is, that we become immobile and default to people we think are experts. But God does not go searching for perfection. Moses was far from perfect. God's plan includes everyone.

In the not-so-distant past, I was eagerly preparing for a much-anticipated sabbatical. Months before it was to start, I created an agenda to fulfill the goals I had set in my sabbatical proposal, complete with a reading list and expected writing projects on the subject-typical scholarly work, with plenty of reading and writing ahead of me.

Not surprisingly, the weeks didn't unfold as expected. It didn't even start as expected. Midway through my last day in the office before sabbatical was to begin, I was escorted to the ER for emergency surgery, which kicked off several months of chaos. Another scheduled surgery, adoptions, baptisms, and family crisis after crisis kept popping up. Change was happening faster that I could keep up. My husband and I were trying to head up a four-generation household that felt like it was in constant crisis. It soon dawned on me that my sabbatical was not going to be about my vocation as a teacher. The needs of the household became the priority. My sabbatical agenda for my vocation would have to wait.

But that is where I got it all wrong. As I reflected on that time in my life, I began to realize that focusing on the relationships in my household was not about putting my vocation aside. Those relationships in this particular place was my vocation as much as any other role and place I find myself. I had been operating under the assumption that vocation, by definition, was how we served God in this world through our jobs, careers, titles, roles, and in specific places. However, the experiences in my life during sabbatical began to shape a new definition of vocation for me. That definition moved from vocation as that thing we do, or strive to do, to who we are, our very being, and ultimately what it means to be human. Ultimately, vocation is how we live out the many systems and circles of relationships in our lives wherever our place might be.

Dietrich Bonhoeffer, in his book *Sanctorum Communio*, states that "individuals exist only in relation to an 'other.' . . . For the individual to exist 'others' must be there."[3] As much as we try, vocation cannot be separated from our relationships. Vocation, by definition, is how I choose to live within those relationships, which includes those in and outside of my home. Vocation then is not the job we have in ministry, but how we live our lives in relation to all of creation, especially in the ordinary, everydayness of life, in the places and communities of our lives, old and new.

Relationship

> *Then he said, "Come no closer! Remove the sandals from your feet, for the place on which you are standing is holy ground." He said further, "I am the God of your father, the God of Abraham, the God of Isaac, and the God of Jacob." And Moses hid his face, for he was afraid to look at God.*[4]

Though just a few short sentences, these verses are pivotal to Moses' call story. Here God lays out the nature of their relationship. "I am . . . , I am . . . , I am . . . ," makes it clear to Moses who God is before any ministry instructions are given concerning what Moses is to do. In fact, the only directives in these verses are related to the relationship they will have, not the tasks at hand. "Remove the sandals from your feet, for the place on which you are standing is holy ground," says the angel. Holy ground. How would it change our

3. Bonhoeffer, *Sanctorum Communio*, 51.

4. Exod 3:5–6 NRSV.

understanding of the nature of this relationship if the reason Moses needed to remove his sandals wasn't to separate himself from God, but to draw closer to God by digging his toes in the sand?[5]

Culturally, we have understood holy as being removed from or set apart. We have created the great divide between the divine and secular, the holy and human. But what if we have it all wrong? What if the holiness of God is not about separating ourselves from God (as if we could ever actually do that) but to draw us closer in? Kaitlin Curtice, in her book *Glory Happening*, states that divinity is found in the everyday, ordinariness of life—and, I would add, our relationships: "In that space, our timelines become stories, and our stories become glory-truth for each other, in our deepest hurts and in our most joyous celebrations, because *glory* is about paying attention in every space and season-glory is about magnificence."[6]

There are some relationships that have a more prominent place in our lives. Let's call them primary relationships. We all have those kinds of relationships, the ones that fill our life (or drain our life depending on the day). They shape our days, our time, our worldview, maybe even our understanding of God. Mothering is one such example—a role that can be both a blessing and a curse. There is nothing else in the world that brings more joy and simultaneously sucks every ounce of energy from you. But to understand this vocationally is not to see it as a thing one does, or a thing one even chooses to do. It just is.

What I have come to realize as I reflect on the many "mothering" relationships in my life is that I do not take care of children. I do not possess children or "have" children. I relate to children. And I am in relationship differently with different children. Some of those relationships are described with words like mother, parent, caregiver, or grandmother. But even these words are limiting. To be fair, some of my children have many mothers. They have adopted mothers and birth mothers, grandmothers and godmothers.

5. I give credit for this insight to a young woman in campus ministry who spent time with me and her colleagues dwelling in this text one early Saturday morning.

6. Curtice, *Glory Happening*, xii.

Some have had foster mothers and stepmothers. While titles may describe the structural place each one of these women has in their lives, they do not describe the functioning relationship.[7] Titles are not the same as vocation. If vocation is how we stand before God in God's creation, these relationships then inform how we stand before God. Who we are in relation to God cannot be understood outside of how we relate to all of creation, including children. Dare I say that how we reflect on these relationships and the presence of these people in our lives may even change how we see and understand God, and our understanding of who God is may even change how we live into these relationships?

What if we stopped thinking about children, people, relationships, communities, or even creation as things we have, or own? What if we started using different language—language that is not about power, control, or ownership?

Douglas John Hall suggests, in an article he wrote for the *Journal for Preachers*, as an alternative to power, the idea of stewardship.[8] The gospel, he says, offers an alternative to the way of power as love, whereby stewardship provides us a way of "making love concrete and practical in our time."[9] To explain what he means he offers three points:

- Stewardship is the way of participation, not domination. A steward is a member of the community she or he serves. *The way of the steward is the way of participation in the general human condition. Stewardship is a way of making good our membership in the human race, of serving our fellow creatures, of deliberately participating in our creaturely state.*
- Stewardship is about trusteeship, not possession or ownership. Who really owns the land? The water? Does the way we carry out our responsibilities change when we care for someone or something that doesn't belong to us?

7. Thanks to Diana Garland for her work in differentiating between structural and functional familial roles in *Family Ministry: A Comprehensive Guide*.

8. Hall, "On Being Stewards," 18–23.

9. Hall, "On Being Stewards," 20.

- Stewardship is that of accountability. It means to *be* accountable, to be accountable to someone greater than ourselves. It means to be accountable to our fellow human beings, the very people we are called to serve and to the One who created.

While Hall's article argued primarily for stewardship as an alternative to political power, I propose that it has implications for how we understand relationships as well. Participation not domination, trusteeship not possession or ownership, accountability not mastery. What would it look like if we took seriously our place in relationship as stewards, not owners, as reflections of God, not ourselves? I think about how that may change my expectations for my children and the other relationships in my life. How might it change our way of thinking about not only setting expectations, but leave-taking and saying goodbye, or hospitality and saying hello? After all, that which we are called to steward is not ours to keep indefinitely. Stewarding is about welcoming and letting go.

Invitation

> *Then the Lord said, "I have observed the misery of my people who are in Egypt; I have heard their cry on account of their taskmasters. Indeed, I know their sufferings, and I have come down to deliver them from the Egyptians, and to bring them up out of that land to a good and broad land, a land flowing with milk and honey, to the country of the Canaanites, the Hittites, the Amorites, the Perizzites, the Hivites, and the Jebusites. The cry of the Israelites has now come to me; I have also seen how the Egyptians oppress them."*[10]

When God calls us, God invites us to join in what God is already doing. God is not this far-off God that sits, watches, and waits. Note the subject of all of the sentences in these verses. "I have observed . . . , I have heard . . . , I know . . . , I have come down . . ." God is laying it all out for Moses. This is about what God is *already* doing, and God is inviting Moses to join God in this very important work.

10. Exod 3:7–9 NRSV.

In the last decade a major longitudinal study was completed by Christian Smith (National Study on Youth and Religion) and his colleagues looking at the religious and spiritual lives of teenagers across the country.[11] It almost entirely dispelled the myth that teenagers were not spiritual or religious. What was interesting was not so much the fact that they were religious, but for those who identified as Christians, how they described God. For them God was some far-off cosmic butler, who stood by and watched the world go by. Our relationship to God was to go about our business, live good moral lives until we needed help, then we could "ring God up." The fancy name Smith and his researchers gave for this understanding of God is Moralistic Therapeutic Deism. Except, this isn't the God in Christ that we know—Immanuel, God with us. We confess our faith in a God that is present, in the here and now. God is before us, with us, and after us, every step of the way, not just waiting by the side for us to call but actively engaging in the world.

When we talk about God inviting us, God is not asking us to do something *for* God, but to do something *with* God. When Jesus says, in the very last verse of Matthew, "And remember, I am with you always, to the end of the age," [12] he isn't spouting a platitude. I hear the promise very literally: "You will receive power when the Holy Spirit comes on you."[13]

Where do we start in this joining God? We start by living out our vocation, by loving all of creation and its creatures (great and small) with our whole hearts through the many calls in our lives.

Call

> *"So come, I will send you to Pharaoh to bring my people, the Israelites, out of Egypt." But Moses said to God, "Who am I that I should go to Pharaoh, and bring the Israelites out of Egypt?" He said, "I will be with you; and this shall*

11. Smith and Denton, *Soul Searching*.
12. Matt 28:20 NRSV.
13. Acts 1:8 NRSV.

> *be the sign for you that it is I who sent you: when you have brought the people out of Egypt, you shall worship God on this mountain.*"[14]

Finally, we get to the actual call. In these last three verses we finally get to hear what God wants Moses to do. He is to go to Pharaoh and bring God's people out of Egypt. Call is not your job, role, or title. Those things are used to help describe your call. Call is how you live out one piece of your vocation at a specific point in time, in a particular place in your life. Calls change over time. We can have more than one call at any point in time. In fact, we usually are called in several ways at the same time. I am called to be a teacher, wife, mother, administrator, and so on. Calls can be short-term or take a lifetime. Some calls do not change, but the nature of the relationships can change over time (i.e., I am a parent—how I parent my toddler is different than how I parent my young adult son, but living out my call as a parent doesn't stop).

Boundaries become crucial in helping all of this make sense in our lives. We put boundaries in place to determine the nature of those relationships and help us define our calls within our broader vocation. Boundaries help us to identify what is or is not acceptable in any given relationship. The boundaries I have in place for my relationship with my husband are very different than the boundaries I have with students. My vocation calls me to love and care for them both. Boundaries help me determine how to love and care for them, and how to make sure both of us flourish in the relationship. Brené Brown, in her fabulous book *Braving the Wilderness*, says, "The clearer and more respected the boundaries, the higher the level of empathy and compassion for others."[15] Boundaries are not just to protect the people in relationships. While that is important, they also exist so that relationships can flourish.

There are two things I know for sure about understanding vocation as our multiple calls to live in relationships in and among God's people. First of all, the people of God are everywhere, not just in church and not just in our homes. They exist beyond the

14. Exod 3:10–12 NRSV.

15. Brown, *Braving the Wilderness*, 70–71.

walls of the church, and they do not wear name tags! The church exists for the people who are not there. And, the church exists for the people that are there. Both need to be tended to.

As we gather together as communities and worship, we are being formed into our identity as children of God together. Remember the last verse of our text, God says you will receive a sign and the promise of that sign is not a conditional statement. That sign is enacted *when* you worship—not *if* you worship. These practices shape and inform whose we are. But whose we are cannot be fully understood through worship alone. Living into our identity as God's people must be seen through the eyes of the people not worshipping with us. These two are not mutually exclusive. It is only through our encounter with others that we can become the people God has created us to be. This is about mutuality. We do not invite people to come to church so they can be like us. We seek out relationships with people, so we can both be transformed. In Christ we are a new creation.

Second, the people of God are each, in their own ways, leaders. Each and every one of us is a leader, each unique and able to contribute. This is the work of the people, not just those rostered, not just those in denominational or judicatory offices, or those with training or degrees. The mission of God involves all leaders in faith communities, not just one or two. These leaders gather together to worship, hear the word of God, and feast at God's table.

What we are talking about is really what it means to be a community of faith. It is a way of thinking about why we are a worshipping community. We do this not for ourselves to build up the church and not just for others at the expense of the church. By joining God in the reconciliation and healing of the world, we are building up the body of Christ and contributing to the church's flourishing, for the sake of the world.

This is where the idea of call can help. Call is the way in which we define a particular relationship. It can come in the form of a title, job, or role that we carry out within our ongoing vocation. Sometimes that may be a job. Jobs come and go, but present within those jobs are opportunities for relationships that require their own boundaries. Sometimes it might be a particularly defined form of relationship, such as supervisor or employee. I am also called to be a neighbor, wife, Sunday School teacher, . . . (fill in the blank). Calls are concrete and practical.

Worshipping communities have callings too. Each is unique, with distinct gifts, emerging in specific places and times. These communities are called into relationships in and through their contexts. They are part of the contexts in which they find themselves. Some worshipping communities set up boundaries to establish an over-and-against type of relationship with their contexts. Others might form more porous boundaries, living in a way of mutuality with their contexts. Whether intentionally defined or not, boundaries exist, and they define a church's relationship with its community. They are called to bear one another and suffer with one another.[16] How they do that is shaped by the boundaries they set in response to their interpretation of call.

Poet Christian Wiman, in his book of essays called *My Bright Abyss*, says,

> The meanings that God calls us to in our lives are never abstract. Though the call may ask us to redefine, or refine what we know as life, it does not demand a renunciation of life in favor of something beyond it. Moreover, the call is always composed of life. That is, not some hitherto unknown voice to which we respond; it is life calling to life.[17]

This is where we come full circle. As one trying desperately to figure out how to be in relationship with the people God has placed in my life, whether they be toddlers that can shimmy up a wall of cabinets faster than you can blink or students in a classroom, hungry to learn more about this God in Christ they profess, I am in a constant state of discernment. Listening deeply for the Holy Spirit's guidance as I live out my vocation of stewarding relationships in such a way that creates space for both of us to discover

16. Scott Hagley does a great job of linking this suffering to call as love in his book, *Eat What Is Set before You*.

17. Wiman, *My Bright Abyss*, 93–95.

how God is calling each of us to live on this earth, amid all the joy, pain, and tears.

However, to end here would mean it were all up to us, but it isn't. It isn't about us, individually. It is about what God is doing in and through us communally. As communities of faith we are called to discern God's presence and work in the world, and discern communally how to prioritize and strengthen the many relationships in our lives. The life of a congregation, then, is not so much the place we go to be nourished (as if it were ever about us) but the place we go to orient—orient our relationships with one another with Christ as the center. My vocation, your vocation, our vocation was, and is, the vocation of the gathered congregation entering into relationships in our lives' ecosystems that are shaped by Christ and shape our understanding of Christ. These relationships are about the local, the people we meet each and every day in the ordinariness of life.

This is the Holy Spirit's work in us, among us, and ahead of us—continually creating, leading, and guiding. Congregations are called to join the Spirit, to live out their vocations as communities in specific times and places. This particularity of context is universal for all congregations and shapes the nature of how communities relate to creation. Each worshipping community bears the privileges of stewarding the relationships it has, which looks, tastes, acts, feels, and sounds different for each. Through this stewarding, congregations open themselves up to a process of transformation, of becoming and being formed, always being made new in Christ. Our identity as church is constantly being formed by the way we engage in relationships individually and communally. We are shaped by our call because God is pulling us forward. Life together, as community and in community, is then not a picture of idealism, but a reality of participation and transformation. Not unlike the primary relationships of our lives (including those that are energy creating and energy depleting) life together in community is always complex and challenging. But even here, perhaps especially here, Christ is present. Through these relationships and within these communities we are a new creation. This is transformation. This is our vocation as church.

8

Forming Generous Disciples

David Loleng

Do not store up for yourselves treasures on earth, . . . but store up for yourselves treasures in heaven . . . for where your treasure is, there your heart will be also.[1]

Do nothing out of selfish ambition and conceit, but in humility regard others as better than yourselves. Let each of you look not to your own interests, but to the interest of others.[2]

In the book *The Paradox of Generosity: Giving We Receive, Grasping We Lose*, Smith and Davidson reflect on the fact that, "although generosity is good for us, generosity is often elusive."[3] Increasing generosity in our new worshipping communities is an ongoing problem. We tend to turn to technical fixes and best practices as the answer, the "silver bullet," to address our vitality and sustainability issues, especially as it relates to financial stewardship and generosity, and specifically as it affects the bottom line, which is our operating budgets. Narrative budgets, E-giving, revamped financial stewardship campaigns, and talking about financial stewardship throughout the

1. Matt 6:19–21 NRSV.
2. Phil 2:3–4 NRSV.
3. Davidson and Smith, *Paradox of Generosity*, 1–10.

year are important and impactful, but I believe they are not enough to bring about lasting transformation in people and in the culture of our worshipping communities. Instead, we should aim to form generous disciples of Jesus who join in Christ's mission in our world. So how can we increase generosity (time, talent, and resources) in our new worshipping communities?

In order to address the vitality and sustainability of our worshipping communities, we need to make a fundamental paradigm shift from focusing on funds development to focusing on people development, or formation. Forming generous disciples should be at the core of our faith community's vitality and sustainability. To put it another way, we need to measure our success not by the quality of our programs but by the qualities that make for a generous community.

One of the most effective ways to form generous disciples of Christ and stewards of all God has provided to us is by creating habits and practices that will begin to change our beliefs and behaviors. It is not just the occasional generous act but sustained practices, disciplines, and a lifestyle of generosity that will have a transformative and lasting effect on individuals and our faith communities.

In Matthew 6:19–21, Jesus connects stewardship to the human heart. What we treasure reveals and shapes the state of our heart. John Westerhoff says it this way: "*Stewardship* is everything we do after we say, 'we believe.'"[4] *Stewardship* includes what we do with the time, resources, and talents/gifting—including our passions, creativity, reasoning, and bodies—that God has generously placed into our care to be used for Christ's mission and purposes in our communities and world. If we want generosity for people instead of just from people, the question becomes: what spiritual practices will help cultivate generosity and Christ-centered stewardship in our worshipping communities, and in so doing, allow our worshipping communities to join in Christ's mission where God has placed and called us? Although there are several practices that we could point to that will help to form generous disciples,

4. Westerhoff, *Grateful and Generous Hearts*, 7.

two spiritual practices in particular help form communities into habits and postures of generosity: practicing simplicity and observing margins.

Two Disciplines: Practicing Simplicity and Margin

Practicing Simplicity

As a spiritual discipline, simplicity helps us to let go of our inordinate attachment to things and our insatiable desire for more. Our culture has convinced us that we need more, better, newer, faster, and sooner. We want a better home, fine furnishings, a vacation that will top the last one that we can post on social media, the newest car or smart phone, the latest fashions, faster internet, more cable channels, and on and on it goes. It is estimated that an average person in America is bombarded by over five thousand advertisements each day. A simple Amazon search with the key words "simple living," will return more than one hundred thousand items, from books to products one could purchase to live more simply. Contemporary life has convinced our society that we need these things to be content. Unbridled consumerism and acquisition of things has even spawned new vocabulary words like *retail therapy* and *affluenza* to describe it. That's why Ecclesiastes 5:10 (NRSV) warns, "The lover of money will not be satisfied with money; nor the lover of wealth with gain. This also is vanity."

The abundant life, we seem to think, is about getting *more*—more of anything that can be better, newer, faster, and in our hands sooner. The anxious urge to consume now and pay later is fed by a sense of scarcity. Simplicity addresses the power of avarice and greed that is so prevalent in our culture of acquiring and materialism. Simplicity helps to unclutter our lives of excess and practice things like frugality, contentment, thankfulness, graciousness, selflessness, and generosity.

Richard Foster describes the importance of simplicity in his book *Freedom of Simplicity: Finding Harmony in a Complex World*, writing,

> The complexity of rushing to achieve and accumulate more and more threatens frequently to overwhelm us. . . . Christian simplicity . . . brings sanity to our compulsive extravagance, and peace to our frantic spirit. . . . It allows us to see material things for what they are—goods to enhance life, not to oppress life. People once again become more important than possessions. . . . It is the Spiritual Discipline of simplicity that gives us . . . a strategy of action that can address this [poverty and hunger] and many other social inequities.[5]

Why then is practicing simplicity so difficult? I believe it has to do with our mindset and worldview. We need to change our behaviors and our beliefs. We need to shift from a mindset and theology of *scarcity* to a mindset and theology of *sufficiency*. A mindset and theology of scarcity is one of the reasons we consume more than we need. Our sense of scarcity is driven by myths that we believe to be true. First is the myth that more is better. Another myth is the belief that there will not be enough for everyone and we will be left out in the cold. This goes against the biblical theology of God's sufficiency, that out of God's abundance there is enough for everyone's need.

Sometimes we contrast scarcity with a term like abundance. However, focusing on abundance by itself can lead to a nuanced form of prosperity gospel, which misleadingly attributes material scarcity to a lack of faith. In *The Soul of Money*, Lynne Twist writes:

> Sufficiency . . . is not the same as abundance (abundance is more than we need—it is excess). Sufficiency is precise. It means that things are sufficient, exactly enough. There is a principle of sufficiency, and it is as follows: When you let go of trying to get more of what you don't really need, which is what we are all trying

5. Foster, *Freedom of Simplicity*, 80–81.

> to get more of, it frees up immense energy to make a difference with what *you* have.[6]

We know, for example, that there is enough food to sustain everyone on the planet, but some consume more than they need. At the center of over consumption is the belief that what I have is mine to use however I want, usually for my own gain and pleasure. Philippians 2:3–4 challenges that false narrative. The truth is quite simple, all we have comes from and ultimately belongs to God (as Ps 24:1 affirms), and it should be used not just for my needs but also for the benefit of others and for the common good.

Enough trusts in God's sufficiency like manna in the wilderness. When God's people wandered from Egypt to the promised land, they were fearful that there would not be enough food to sustain them. But God provided *manna* as food to sustain them. The catch was that they were not supposed to store the *manna* for longer than a day, and if they did it would spoil. They were taught the lesson that God would supply their needs, but they had to rely on God's sufficiency every day to provide enough. Each, in the end, gathered as much as she or he needed.[7]

The practice of simplicity and adopting a theology of sufficiency helps us to recalibrate our lives back toward God and God's will. Simplicity helps us to enter into a posture of trust that God cares for us and will provide for us sufficiently. It is not focused on minimalism or the *tidying* craze that is currently in vogue.[8] Simplicity addresses the power we give to objects. We give them power: over our identity; over our sense of security; over our dreams and passions. We place all these things under God's power and trust in God's sufficient grace and ability to provide for our needs. Simplicity frees us to be generous with our money and resources, and allows us to be more missionally focused. Richard Foster reminds us that "the goal of work is not

6. Twist, *Soul of Money*, Kindle loc. 1001, 1236–43, 3756.

7. Exod 16:18 NRSV.

8. See Kondo, *Life-Changing Magic of Tidying Up*.

to gain wealth and possessions, but to serve the common good and bring glory to God."[9]

Practicing Margin

The second spiritual practice, creating *margins* in life, is connected to simplicity. Just as simplicity helps us to let go of our inordinate attachment to things, creating margins allows us to let go of our inordinate attachment to our schedules and busyness. Simply put, simplicity and margins help us to unclutter our lives so that we can make space for the other, for God and for God's kingdom purposes.

As Richard Swenson describes in his book *Margin*, margin is like the space on this page that you are reading, there is no text on the top, bottom, and sides, just empty space. Swenson goes on to describe what being marginless is like when he writes:

> The condition of modern-day living devours margin. . . . Marginless is being thirty minutes late to the doctor's office because you were twenty minutes late out of the hairdresser's because you were ten minutes late dropping the kids off at school because. . . .[10]

In *The Good and Beautiful God*, James Bryan Smith writes, "We add so much to our schedules that we have no 'margin,' no space for leisure and rest and family and God and health."[11] Margin addresses one of the enemies of our soul, which is *hurry*. John Ortberg tells a story about the time he had just arrived at a church right outside Chicago, a very large and globally known church. He wanted to start well so he called his mentor Dallas Willard and asked him what advice he had for him as he started work at his new call. John was expecting several wise words and helpful directions from his mentor. After a long silence on the phone, Dallas Willard said this to him, "John, you must ruthlessly eliminate hurry from your life." John said his first reaction was, "Is that it?"

9. Foster, *Freedom of Simplicity*, Kindle loc. 2372/3665.

10. Swenson, *Margin*, 32.

11. Smith, *Good and Beautiful God*, 128.

He would come to realize just how wise and perceptive that advice was for the rest of his ministry and life.[12] Ruthlessly eliminate hurry from your life. So simple, but so difficult for many of us. Why? It's because, as Smith argues, "we live in a culture that rewards *busyness* and overextension as signs of importance."[13] This is true not only of the culture around us but also in our fast moving, entrepreneurial, worshipping community and church planting culture. The busier we are, and the more plates we are juggling, the more "stuff" we are doing, the more hours we are working, the more exhausted we are, and the more important and valued we feel. We not only feel this from people in our lives, but we also feel we are more important and valuable to God because of how much we do, how hurried we are, how busy we are, all for the furthering of God's reign. Practicing *margin* is imperative not only for our ministries but also for our souls.

So how do we practice *margin*? It starts with saying no: "Saying no to anything that is not absolutely necessary to the well-being of your soul or the welfare of others."[14] If we took time to look at all we do in a week we could likely identify things that we could say no to. We need to constantly remind ourselves that when we say no to something, we are actually saying yes to something else. It is difficult for many of us because often the choice is not between a good thing or a bad thing, it is usually between two good things. It is important to make a distinction between *margin* and *creating boundaries*. Creating boundaries is about "drawing a line in the sand," creating margin is for the sake of making space in your life. Thus, margin means creating extra space in our lives, decluttering our schedules, time, and lives. When we live with margin, we can be more generous with our time, talents, and relationships.

Margin is also a practice that can be implemented in our worshipping communities. How are we practicing margin in our worship services? Do we allow space for God to speak to people or the community during our time of gathered worship?

12. Ortberg, "Ruthlessly Eliminate Hurry."

13 Smith, *Good and Beautiful God*, 129.

14. Smith, *Good and Beautiful God*, 129.

Are we so inward focused that we are cluttering church life with too many activities and programs? Or are we encouraging those in our churches / worshipping communities to spend more time with others who are not yet part of our churches / worshipping communities? Creating margin positively affects our relationship with God and others, our health and our ability to join in Christ's mission in our communities and world.

A Lived Theology

Dorothy Bass and Craig Dykstra define practices in relationship to the Christian faith in the following way: "Christian practices address fundamental human needs and conditions . . . and they do so in ways that reflect God's purposes for humankind. . . . Normatively and theologically understood, therefore, Christian practices are the human activities through which people cooperate with God in addressing the needs of others and creation."[15] Based on this definition, simplicity and margin are Christian practices meant to form generous disciples. It is important to understand that these practices are not just an end unto themselves or even a way to gain favor with God. These practices, and others like them, illuminate what we believe about God and God's mission in the world. They offer a lived theology. By practicing simplicity and margin, we perform a theology of God's abundance and sufficiency toward us. We are also reflecting on God's desire that we use the resources entrusted to us for the common good.

What we discover from practices like simplicity and margin is that they actually address the deep longing in our souls for the abundant life that Jesus speaks about in John 10:10. It is abundance that is different from the lifestyle of abundance and over-abundance that our society offers. What we need is to practice "ways of life that are abundant, not in things but in love, justice and mercy."[16] Therefore, these Christian practices, and others are

15. Bass and Dykstra, "Practicing Theology," 21–22.

16. Bass and Dykstra, "Practicing Theology,"16.

ongoing ways in which we try to live a biblically abundant and generous way of life.

The spiritual disciplines of simplicity and margin not only help to cultivate a culture of generosity, but help form people in our worshipping communities who are growing as generous disciples of Jesus Christ, with a greater impact on our communities and world. What might be a few other spiritual practices/disciplines that you could incorporate into your life and the lives of those who are a part of your worshipping community?

Christ-centered stewardship and generosity are difficult. Adam Copeland says that "stewardship is both simple and complex . . . it's complex because consumerist tendencies and cultural norms often draw our focus away from God. Like much of our faith, stewardship can be not only countercultural but also counterintuitive. After all, how can it be that in giving things away we ultimately discover wealth."[17] I want to image and imitate God's generosity. It begins with surrender: to surrender all that I have and all that I am so that God can form me into a more generous disciple of Jesus Christ and to live my life as a witness to others of the very generous character of the God we serve. Do you desire this as well? Do you desire this for your worshipping community?

17. Copeland, introduction to *Stewardship 101*, 2.

Section 3

Leadership Development in a Sustainable Church Ecology

9

Democratizing Church Planting

Entrepreneurship as an Act of Discipleship for the Whole Church

MICHAEL MOYNAGH

AS I REFLECT ON the emergence in the UK of "fresh expressions of church" (often called new worshipping communities), I am struck by an evolution in how we understand them. This evolution has implications for stewarding both their leadership and the church's resources.

From Church Planting to Discipleship

The evolution began with church-growth-driven church planting.[1] Church plants tended to replicate existing models of church. They often attracted mainly recent or current churchgoers who were disenchanted with the church. And they relied on large-ish planting teams. The priority was to grow the team, so that it became big enough to launch a public congregation.

1. Paas, *Church Planting*, 37–38.

However, during the 1990s some churchgoers began to form Christian communities with people well outside the church, on a "we will make it up as we go" basis. These communities frequently looked different compared to existing congregations. They were more focused on people outside the church than conventional church plants, and each was initiated by a relatively small Christian core.

They were observed and interpreted largely against the background of church-growth-based church planting. Stuart Murray, who theologized about them, George Lings, who told some of their stories, and Bob and Mary Hopkins, who coached and encouraged many of them, all came from church-planting backgrounds.[2] The *Mission-Shaped Church* report (2004), which did much to stimulate these "fresh expressions," was written by a group that was asked to update the Church of England's church planting guidelines.

As a result, these new worshipping communities were initially seen as better contextualized church plants.[3] In particular, immediately following the report there was a tendency to think that multiplying these communities required, like church planting, full or part-time paid leaders who had special gifts for the task. Such leaders have played an important role. However, it has become increasingly apparent that many "ordinary" Christians have also been starting these communities in their spare time, as part of their discipleship.

This includes clergy who have done so amid their other responsibilities. One Church of England minister, for example, has recently birthed a community for families who enjoy board games. These families are then invited to "Lego Heroes," where they hear a Bible story and make Lego models to illustrate it. Christian formation begins as families discuss what they are making. What is striking about this and similar examples is that typically they don't need ministers to start them: lay people can do something similar.

2. E.g., Murray, *Church after Christendom*; *Post-Christendom*; *Changing Mission*. Lings edited the Encounters on the Edge series, published by Church Army, Sheffield. However, Moynagh, *Changing World*, wrote from a more postmodern perspective, as did others in what was then known as the emerging church conversation.

3. In 2008, Murray titled his updated textbook *Church Planting*.

Indeed, many have. Tim met with a group of young adults who were dissatisfied with church. They advertised free canoeing on the weekend and paid for the canoes. Families (most of whom did not attend church) canoed together and socialized afterward. As they ate and talked together, someone would tell the children a Bible story, with the adults listening in. Noticing hearers' curiosity, Tim invited those interested to "food and story" on Tuesday evenings. A small group gathered (while the weekend canoeing continued). Tim introduced them to Discovery Bible Study based on four questions:

- If this story happened today, what would it look like?
- What is the story saying to you?
- Could the story make a difference to your life and if so, how?
- (A week later) Did the story make a difference to your life and if so, how?

The group continues to meet as it journeys toward Jesus.

Louisa was a community nurse. She knew that an unusually large number of mothers in the area suffered from postpartum depression. With two friends, she decided to host a weekly drop-in center. Later it became apparent that the mothers would enjoy meeting together without their children, while their partners stayed with the kids. So, three in the group started discussion evenings using a video about lives that had been changed by God. Gradually, the group evolved into a church. Ten years later, I met one of the original mothers at a Christian conference, and another at a different Christian conference!

As we have observed these initiatives, it is becoming clear that the Spirit is unleashing a twenty-first century way of following Jesus. It involves prayerfully:

- Finding one or more friends in a walk of your life.
- Listening to your own interests and passions, the people you know, and to God.
- Discerning a simple, regular way to love people around you.

- Deepening relationships with the people who are drawn to your practical love.
- Sharing the Christian faith appropriately as opportunities arise.
- Encouraging people found by God to form a worshipping community where they are, in the midst of their everyday lives, and to connect it to the wider church.
- Helping new Christians to repeat the process among their friends.

These and other examples invite us to see new worshipping communities less as expressions of church planting, and more as a form of discipleship. The latter resonates more easily with church members. Appeals based on averting church decline or enabling the church to join God's mission can often feel abstract and remote from Christians' ordinary lives. By contrast, discovering new ways to follow Jesus makes a more direct connection, and does justice to what we are observing.

This approach to discipleship enables Christians to be better stewards of the worlds they inhabit. Their love goes beyond warm feelings and nice conversations. It becomes organized, which is frequently necessary for love. Think of a family: getting the children to school, the evening meal, a birthday party, weekend activities, a family treat, and many other acts of love have to be organized. It helps obviously to organize them with someone else. (Of course, many single parents do so brilliantly, but most of them would prefer a mate.)

Organization is much easier—and more fun—when it is done by two or more people together. This revolutionizes day-to-day discipleship. Following Jesus stops being an individualistic affair and becomes collaborative. In particular, when Christians jointly organize practical love, their capacity to bring a fuller life to others is greatly enhanced. They are more able to steward what is wholesome in the context and add to it.

As people gravitate to this organized love, Christians can take the opportunity to pass on the most valuable gift they have ever received—communal life with Jesus. This is the heart of grace: not an individualistic experience, despite the importance of personal response, but community with Christ. Yet how can Christians offer this community on their own? They can invite people to Sunday church, of course. But many congregations meet at a time and place, with a style and an agenda that make them inaccessible to others. The person invited may have family commitments on Sunday, or live too far away, or find the worship style culturally off-putting, or not identify with worshipping Christ.

A more realistic alternative is to offer, as part of a fuller life, Christian community to people where they are, in their everyday lives, starting with listening and love. This gift can best be offered by Christians who are themselves a community, however small. They comprise the core of the new worshipping community and link it to the church at large. Instead of merely consuming the church, they pass it on. They become multipliers of what they have received. Thereby Christians become more fruitful stewards of not only the world, but the church.

Stewarding Leadership

This has implications for how twenty-first century disciples are supported. If ordinary Christians can start new communities in their daily lives, what happens to the traditional church planting assumption that planters need specific skills and character traits?

Such a view seems anachronistic in light of research into secular entrepreneurs. After decades of effort, there is still no consensus on the skills and personality traits associated with entrepreneurial success. Self-efficacy—a person's belief that they can successfully perform the tasks in hand—is the one characteristic that does stand out.[4] But is self-efficacy something you are born with or a characteristic that is revealed in the right circumstances?

Chen, Greene, and Crick suggest that many people may shun entrepreneurial activities not because they lack the necessary skills, but because they think they do—they lack self-efficacy. An

4. Moynagh, *Church in Life*, 311.

environment perceived to be supportive of entrepreneurship will increase entrepreneurial self-efficacy because individuals assess their entrepreneurial capacities in reference to perceived resources, opportunities, and obstacles in the environment. Personal efficacy is more likely to be developed and sustained in a supportive environment than in an adverse one.[5]

David Rae speculates that entrepreneurial ability may be more widespread in the general population than is often realized. It remains latent because circumstances do not draw it out. Trying to specify entrepreneurial traits may create stereotypes that potential entrepreneurs do not identify with. It wrongly suggests that only a minority can be entrepreneurial. Potential entrepreneurs are put off.[6] Might there be lessons here for church planting?

Caroline, a school teacher in London, knew that many of her children's mothers could not speak English well. So, with volunteers from her church, she started a weekly language cafe. The mothers sat around small tables, enjoyed afternoon tea, and practiced their English. Later, while the cafe continued, a small group met at another time of the week to explore the Christian faith. Caroline said that she used to think of herself as someone in the church with gifts. Leading the language cafe made her realize that she was also able to start something new. She would never have dreamed of putting herself forward to be a "church planter." But here she was, confounding expectations.

Supporting—or "stewarding"—people like Caroline requires a rather different approach to the church's normal select-train-deploy model. Traditionally, individuals are selected, trained, and then released into a predictable form of service. This made sense when the type of church people were being called to start or serve was reasonably clear. However, many new worshipping communities are unpredictable and extremely diverse, which means the skills to start one also vary. It is much harder to anticipate the gifts founders need. Indeed, trying to do so risks turning founders into experts. They have particular characteristics, recognized through

5 Chen et al., "Entrepreneurial Self-Efficacy," 313–14.

6. Rae, *Entrepreneurship*, 28–29.

selection and honed by training, that predispose them to succeed once deployed. Ordinary people may be deterred from starting a community as part of their day-to-day discipleship—"I can't do that. I'm not trained."

Yet, surely these communities are birthed in a relational manner? In which case, isn't the ability to relate well to others a capacity that can be identified in advance? One founder described how he was on the autistic spectrum. "People like me," he said, "don't like meeting face to face." Then he showed me a series of text messages on his phone, "This is my church." On a conventional view, he might not have satisfied the relational criterion. Yet he was exactly the right person to form a worshipping community among people who did not enjoy meeting together.

Instead of "select, train, and deploy," an "encourage, recognize, and support" approach would fit the unpredictable and varied nature of new worshipping communities. For example, in an emerging Church of England initiative, *FX Greenhouse*, church leaders and members are encouraged to start a new Christian community. They are recognized and supported by being invited to bring their teams into a "Greenhouse."

The teams have a common purpose—to help form and reproduce a worshipping community. They take responsibility for their own, just-in-time learning by accessing a free app with stories, frameworks, and advice.[7] They meet twice a year as a community in which they learn from each other while they do their planning. They support each other between meetings through social media. Skype-based coaching is available when required. Though not the current intention, maybe in time the "recognized" element will become more explicit, perhaps with some sort of bishop's license. It is still in the early days, but might this be the beginnings of one way to sustain, through good stewardship, teams that found new worshipping communities?

7. *FX godsend* is available from any online store. The content can also be accessed via www.fxresourcing.org.

Stewarding the Church's Resources

These developments face the objection: "If our lay people start something new, they won't have time to support what exists now. So won't we deplete the resources available to our current congregations, many of which are already fragile? And won't many of the new worshipping communities be small and fragile too? Wouldn't we have made it harder to sustain the existing church, but without birthing a sustainable alternative—poor stewardship all round?"

One response is to see new worshipping communities as little planets around a "sun" congregation. Maybe there is only one planet at first, but we might pray for more. Sun and planets connect through joint social events, a series of shared study evenings, walking through Holy Week together, combined worship events such as a carol or Easter service, and more. Christians in the new community invite others to some of these events. For example, one member of a knitting-based worshipping community ended up attending Knit and Natter twice a week and its parent church, Trinity, also two times a week.[8] If Knit and Natter comes to the end of its natural life, its members have pathways into an existing congregation. Trinity is strengthened by the trickle of new people.

Sometimes old and new blend together. Sunday attendance at St Luke's Church in central England had dropped to the mid-teens. An energetic, spare-time associate minister gathered up to twenty local people, many of whom did not attend church, in his home on Thursday evenings. They shared food and fun, and did some Bible study. Some of them started coming on Sundays for the first time. Meanwhile, Sunday mornings became more like Thursday evenings. People sat around tables, sermons were more interactive, the liturgy was more informal, and over two years numbers grew to between thirty and forty. It is becoming hard to distinguish those belonging to the Thursday group from those belonging to Sunday. Both gatherings are more robust by blending into each other.

So here is a second response. We might see "mixed economy church" and "blended church" as two ends of a spectrum. In the

8. Dutton, "Unpicking," 46.

mixed economy, the existing congregation and new communities have very distinct identities. Occasionally they do things together, but there is little overlay between the main worship of the parent congregation and of the new community. With blended church, there is far more intermingling between the two. Identities overlap, with a stronger sense of one, overarching identity. Might old and new be more supportive of each other, and so more sustainable, the closer we get to the blended model? And is this not a fruitful way to steward the church's resources: start a new worshipping community, and blend it with the existing church?

Third, should sustainability be our goal? What matters, surely, is not the durability of new worshipping communities but their "generativity"—their ability to generate further worshipping communities. Longevity does not guarantee fruit. Some congregations have existed for many years but no longer appear fruitful. Others are short lived but yield abundant fruit. The Jerusalem church lasted for an historically brief period—till AD 70, when the city was destroyed. Yet it was highly generative. Scores of Jews visited Jerusalem for the major festivals, heard about Jesus, went home, and started Christian communities themselves, as in Cyprus and Cyrene (Acts 11:19–30).

Durability is out of kilter with contemporary people's fluid lives. In our choice-driven society, unexpected opportunities pull people away from existing commitments, and individuals commit for shorter periods. To be contextual, new communities must fit into this changing world by changing too. Their lives may end after a relatively short period. Perhaps the original need is no longer so acute, one or two key members leave, or the meeting place stops being available.

Even so, they can pass on the gene of reproduction to those coming to faith. Leaders can teach the principles of twenty-first-century discipleship, and encourage, recognize, and support those who feel called to this manner of life. Though a community may appear to have died, it will continue in the life of its offspring. The community will be sustained, not by being durable, but by generating further communities.

Generativity better suits a society on the move than longevity, which comes from a more static era. It does more to steward the church's resources than clinging to what the church has got at the risk of being sterile. It also resonates with our humanity. The church can be sustained in the same way that the human race is sustained.

Conclusion

It is time, therefore, to democratize church planting. Let the Spirit free it from the clutches of an aristocratic band of gifted specialists. Put it into the hands of ordinary Christians, as part of their twenty-first-century discipleship. Let them find one or more friends, organize practical love, start new worshipping communities in the nooks and crannies of life, and become better stewards of the world and the church. Let the church be a good steward of these everyday leaders. Encourage, recognize, and support them. And pray for a generative outcome in which more breeds more, not mainly for the sake of the church, but primarily as a form of stewardship for the world.

Let the church give itself away. By doing so, it will be faithful to its foundational meal. A piece of the congregation is broken off, and offered as the body of Christ to people outside the church. As they gather round, they receive the gift, consume it in their own way, and are transformed. Then they repeat the process. Thus, Holy Communion-like, the body is passed from one context to another, and from one generation to the next. A new community achieves longevity through its ongoing life in the community it begets. Sustainability occurs through the church's self-donation.

10

Stewardship of Gifts

Discerning and Employing the Human Resources at Our Disposal

Beth Scibienski

Our Story

I had just returned from sabbatical, I was rested and ready for what was next. Upon my arrival, I learned that a local dance school which had been renting space in our building for $14,000 per year had outgrown our building and was leaving for a larger facility. Like many churches, we were dependent on this extra income. Also like many churches, we wondered about our role as a "landlord." Certainly, the church is in the real estate business, and sometimes investing in real estate makes sense. Without question, brick-and-mortar buildings are a blessing and a grace. Ask anyone who sets up worship week after week in a borrowed room! But being responsible for brick and mortar, financially and physically, can be, as Scott Hagley said in the first chapter, "a grace . . . deadened by ideological boredom." Was being a landlord something to which God had called us or was this an easy answer to a larger question: How does a vital congregation make ends meet?

Every church context is unique and the answer to that question needs to be faithful to that unique context. For us, we are a diverse, dynamic congregation in Central New Jersey. It is a diverse place, ethnically, socially, economically, and financially. While our congregation is primarily Caucasian, the community around us was becoming a suburb primarily of immigrant neighbors from all over the world.

We have 130 official members, with a weekly average attendance of 75. We enjoy different kinds of music with an active choir, an active band, a violinist, a flutist, and a concert pianist. We have three or four active small groups. We like one another. We laugh together, even in worship! We are a vibrant congregation, but making ends meet is still hard for us. Raising money for our budget gets harder and harder each year. We worked hard to talk about stewardship of our financial resources. I attended a seminar by the author of *Not Your Parent's Offering Plate*. The issue of making ends meet needs to be about more than meeting our financial needs. But we spend the most time working on getting people to give more, as if that's the only answer.

The Barna Group reported in September 2017 on the differences in understanding generosity in America. They asked Christians in America to rate their preferred method of generosity: service, emotional/relational support, financial gifts, or hospitality.[1] They found that across age ranges, financial gifts were not as urgent as other priorities. But the changes we are seeing in church attendance and financial giving point to a trend beyond the church. They are part of broader changes in the American culture, something Robert Putnam called the collapse of American community.[2]

So much of our culture has changed, and we need to consider wholesale changes to how we do church in response. This is some of the backdrop for why I wanted our elders to consider whether we are called to be landlords. I saw this as a liminal space. A liminal space is the time between *what was* and *what will be*. It seems

1. Barna Group, "Generations & Generosity."
2. Putnam, *Bowling Alone*, title page.

like the answer to those questions is found in, "What is God up to?" In that case, any space can be liminal, can't it?

When faced with a $14,000 deficit, I asked my elders to take one month to discern how God would have us spend our resources: both our building and our gifts within our community. I asked the elders to join me in asking God whether we were to rent our space or perhaps use it in another way to serve the community.

We prayed. Or we dreamed. Same thing.

The dream, the prayer, started to form in my mind. I thought about how we run a preschool that serves eighty families in our neighborhood. We are comfortable using our building for purposes other than worship. I started to think about the members in my congregation. What were their passions and concerns? What was their expertise? What were their skills? What were their careers? What were their interests? Did we have people in the financial sector? People who build things or fix things? Farmers and gardeners? Amateur chefs? Teachers? Social workers? Medical professionals?

There were some trends. Some pockets of folks seemed to work in industries that complimented each other. At this time in the history of our congregation, we happened to have collected a lot of folks in the health and healing industry: a physician, a nurse, a therapist, a yoga instructor, massage therapists, and a life coach.

I gathered them together for lunch and asked, "If it were up to us around this table, what kind of social enterprise could we start in our church building?"

This group of people dreamed of a Wellness Center, a place that offers multiple services to the community promoting health in body, mind, and spirit. They envisioned "vendors" or "providers" using our building to offer classes and services that promote wellness. In exchange for inexpensive rent, we would expect the providers to offer affordable services with a special eye for certain demographics who are underserved.

We needed to present a plan to our elders. We needed a business plan, and I had never created one before. I searched the Internet for "how to start a business." There were several options for creating a business plan. I used *Rocketlawyer* because it was free for the first three months. This particular website fed us a series of questions that helped us gather demographic information, create a financial strategy, and describe our business clearly.[3] The end result was an amazing business plan that made us look like we were seasoned entrepreneurs.

But we were not. We were a group of people who knew a certain industry—the wellness industry. It is completely possible, even probable, that your congregation has a group of people who know a different industry. I have wondered what would have happened if I had gathered a lawyer, a police officer, and a teacher? A general contractor, a painter, and a woman who was really gifted at organization? What would have happened if I had gathered a gifted home cook, a day care provider, and a caregiver? One more? How about a mechanic, a Realtor, and a bookkeeper?

Specific Shapes

I have gotten to this point of the story several times with friends and colleagues and they stop me. They want me to realize that I am particularly gifted at seeing trends or connecting what seems like random things. Perhaps that is true. But it is also true that God is present when two or more are gathered in God's name. The image of God is present in every ministry context. And the image of God is unique in every ministry context. Whether a legacy congregation, an underfunded new worshipping community, a vibrant community of faith, or an aging, even dying congregation, God's sustaining grace is present. As the first chapter of this book suggests, our work is often discerning the specific "ecology" needed to nurture the unique image of God that is present when the people of God work and worship together. Nurturing the specific "ecology" is about "working creatively with the cultural and social materials in that place and discerning a shape of life and form of

3. https://www.rocketlawyer.com.

witness." This is often the "slow, relational, and adaptive" work of church planting. It also needs to be the work of legacy churches.

What stands in our way?

Not Good Enough?

The answer all too often sounds like the cherished sentiment, "That is not what we have done in the past." I had never really thought of Peter, in Acts 11, coming back to Jerusalem with the smell of unclean foods on his clothing, but with that image from the introduction, Scott Hagley painted an all-too-familiar scene from any church meeting space anywhere. Innovation in any form calls into question the way we have done it in the past, and if we are calling the past into question, we cannot humanly help but take the question personally.

By suggesting something different, the assumption is that we are indicting the way we have always done it. The new idea somehow judges the old idea as not just obsolete but inferior. And people in the church have given a lot of time, energy, talent, and money toward the things that are now "not good enough." Ouch. The pastoral truth is that whenever the church did whatever the church used to do, that was what God was doing. It was and will always remain a beautiful witness to the image of God in a specific time and space. But all of us know we have aged. None of us are "doing" church the way we used to do it. What we did yesterday was good enough for yesterday but today is not yesterday. Together, we have got to get behind today.

We Could Fail

Fear of failure often stunts a congregation's ability to move forward. You may know the phrase, "You cannot steer a parked car." Well, you cannot move a still congregation. Plus, there is always risk of making a wrong turn and having to turn around, or, worse yet, start all over. That is true with everything in life. Perfectionism is the enemy of productivity. If we need to have everything all together before we move, we will never move.

One of the rooms we use for our Wellness Center has been redecorated or repurposed three times in the last twelve years. First, we imagined it as a "board room" so we got a big table with twelve chairs. Then a few adults thought it would be a great "youth room" so they painted it and bought bean bag chairs. Turns out the teenagers would rather hang out with the rest of the church family during fellowship time than retreat to their colorful space. Now it has a table with chairs and a sofa with chairs. The church uses it for smaller meetings. The Wellness Center uses it for psychotherapy and small groups. The preschool uses it for parent/teacher conferences. Having to change directions is not failure. It's an exhibit of trying something.

Lack of Buy-In

Although I am not a church planter, I have trained several. In fact, of the dozen seminary students that have finished internships with me, half of them are church planters, entrepreneurs, or community organizers. I do not feel comfortable taking credit for their choices but I do feel comfortable claiming what I know they got from me: a woman who has many ideas and a woman who is a natural leader. I can set my sights on a destination and easily gather two handfuls of people who want to go there with me. And at first glance, I suppose the story of the start of our Wellness Center may seem like I had all the answers before we started. I did not. The spiritual genius of the body of Christ is that one person cannot do the whole project. I can do my part. But if the community is not invested in the vision or the direction, the project is destined to be in my case, a one-woman show.

When I can collaborate with people who do not have the same gifts as me, I am able to use my gifts better. When we are all doing what is natural to us, the project seems easy. One of my gifts is having a good idea. Too often, I have a good idea and I start running with it. When in a few strides I realize I am tired and growing bitter, inevitably I look around to see that I am running alone. And going it alone means I am trying to do things that should be done by others, better suited to their gifts; so I learn the lesson of community vision again. I stop. I listen. I learn why folks were not behind me. I learn about what they care about. I find other important issues that I did not see. And I commit to taking the human resources of my congregation more seriously.

Working Together

Doing things alone is so much easier. I know. It takes twice as long to collaborate on a worship service than it does to just put the thing together on my own. Decisions made by committee are tedious and frustrating. Traveling with a group of people is so much slower. Here's the rub: watching someone grow incrementally in their faith because they participated in the creation of a worship service is worth every minute of slow, incremental leadership.

The problem with the parable of the lost sheep is that going after that sheep is incredibly inefficient.[4] It's 1 percent of the flock. And the fluffy thing ran off on its own, after all. Why must I leave the herd to help the one rogue sheep find its way back to the herd? Well, for starters the walk back together is going to be some of the best conversation I will have. Working together, even if it's walking back to the herd together after exploring new territory, is the spiritual genius of the body of Christ. Relationship is where the whole thing comes together, and relationship takes time.

Building relationships often feels incredibly inefficient. Working together takes longer but it is worth it. The role of the leader is not to do the job but to cast a vision. The hardest part of the pastor's job is casting vision. Vision-casting is almost impossible if we are casting it in the wrong direction or casting it against the wind. In starting the Wellness Center, we learned that when we are doing what God wants us to do, the job is easy. The obstacles are few. The road is smooth.

4. See Luke 15 NRSV.

That is not to say that God does not call us to do hard, frustrating, and time-consuming things. What I am saying is that when we cast vision in the direction of the wind, rather than against the wind, our job is easier. It is not the wind that is the problem in casting, it is the direction of the one casting. When I find myself stumbling over obstacles in the path, when I am frustrated by the complaining and misunderstanding that is so often present in community life, I have learned to check my orientation. Am I facing the wrong way? Do I have enough humility and patience to turn around? Or am I going to hold onto my own plan, even if it's wrong?

When I allow myself to stop and look around, I usually find my community is not too far away. I either lost them because I was going too fast or I failed to give good directions. My job was to lead, to shepherd others, to gather people together and move them in a singular direction. That was my job. It was not my job to work alone. Working together is always better.

The church is in a liminal space. We are in between what we were and what we are becoming. The truth remains: we are here together. All of the human resources at our disposal are actually the end that will meet the means. When we take our human resources seriously, we can begin to discern what God is doing. And if we take those resources seriously, we may join God in the work already at hand.

11

Stewardship of Leadership

Stewarding Culture to Uncover Potential

Jeya So

Third-Culture Leaders

When I met my future husband as a fellow student in seminary, neither of us imagined that we would be lead pastors of a local church, let alone starting a new worshipping community. We often marveled at peers who seemed so confident in their calling to serve in established congregations and puzzled at their insider knowledge of how to navigate ecclesial and judicatory institutional systems, since we were both outsiders to the PC(USA). After graduating from seminary and working in a variety of church ministries ranging from preschool to adult ministries for fourteen years, God called us to help plant Anchor City Church in San Diego, for whom we currently serve as lead pastors.

We often describe Anchor City as a third-culture church. Although *third culture* can be defined in many different ways, we describe third-culture people as those who spent their formative years in a culture different from their parents.[1] Third-culture

1. The third-culture experience is not always strictly confined to these parameters. For example, my daughter is a third-generation Korean American

people innately understand what it means to be a part of different cultures simultaneously and have learned to navigate fluidly from one to another. This could be as simple as code-switching in everyday conversation (alternating between two or more languages) or as complex as being a multiethnic, multicultural family and raising multiethnic, multicultural children.

Often, third-culture people feel like they exist in a constant liminal, in-between space. Unfortunately, many experience this liminality primarily in a negative manner—as "neither this, nor that."[2] We believe Jesus can transform our *neither/nor* experience into a *both/and* identity. Christ does not erase our cultural or ethnic heritage but, rather, redeems it. With our confidence firmly placed in the God who calls us to be *more truly* who God created us to be, we can move freely in the power of the Holy Spirit wherever we find ourselves.

This redemption in Christ helps third-culture people realize that their voices *can* and *should* be heard. *Both/and* people can empathize with others who, regardless of their ethnic or cultural backgrounds, are marginalized or feel like outsiders. Third-culture leaders can help us understand that *everyone* comes from and lives in a culture with a unique point of view—even microcultures of neighborhood, work, or family of origin; a point of view that is a gift to God's diverse and creative world.

As a pastor, I have seen the way many third-culture leaders have felt misunderstood or excluded by the church in the United States. I believe the church needs new worshipping communities like Anchor City to embrace and create community for third-culture leaders and, at the same time, to empower and embolden them to speak into the life of and lead the broader church. As Scott Hagley aptly notes in chapter 1, we can view the uncertain liminal space of our post-Christendom culture in a negative light, with anxiety and

who has been raised in the same culture as myself but, in many ways, she identifies with the third-culture experience.

2. My experiences of being told, both tacitly and explicitly through racism and discrimination, that I could never be "American" because of my Korean heritage while also being told during visits to Korea that I was not "Korean" because I had grown up in the United States are, sadly, echoed by many Asian Americans.

hand-wringing about losing "the good old days," or we can greet and discover it as a wide-open future of mission with Christ. Leaning on the wisdom, insight, and experience of third-culture leaders, who navigate liminal spaces daily, will benefit us all.

Third-culture leaders understand what it means to build bridges between disparate people, experiences, and communities. Becoming a bridge for others can often be painful—as the saying goes, bridges get stepped on. Despite the real possibility of pain, this bridge-building potential is an important gift of God we must steward so that we can participate with God in seeking the shalom of our communities and contexts. Third-culture leaders are able to hold in tension the seeming contradictions between dreams of a new future and continuity with the past.[3] As a pastor, I take seriously the call to raise up leaders who faithfully embody this hope.

To develop leaders for today and for the future, we cannot, as Hagley notes in the first chapter, give in to the temptation to double down on what we have done in the past—focusing on performing certain tasks or generating specific, predetermined outcomes. In our post-Christendom, pluralistic, complex, often contradictory culture, we must steward leaders who can practice third-culture principles. The real leadership challenge before us, then, is not creating a better or more efficient "pipeline" but, rather, stewarding and holding space for new dreams to emerge and take root.

Because I believe in the priesthood of all believers (1 Pet 2:5, 9), I strive to pastor a whole church on mission with God. This vision of whole-life discipleship calls each member of our community to be leaders everywhere and anywhere God calls them—wherever we work, live, or play. Stewarding unlikely leaders is a vital part of why we said, and continue to say, *yes* to God's call to plant and pastor a community of humble, generous leaders who simply want to serve God and others. In our context, cultivating

3. For many third-culture leaders, immigration is intertwined in their family and church narratives. Older generations literally left behind their homelands and, in building new lives and new churches in a new land, rely on their third-culture offspring to translate both language and culture for them. Sometimes it seems that established churches and new worshipping communities speak different languages and need "interpreters" to create common understanding.

and developing leaders includes, but is not limited to, stewarding place, pain, and potential.

Stewarding Place

When we talk about stewarding "place," we are not referring to buildings or properties. We often remind our community that church is *people*, not a building. For Anchor City, *place* is about discovering our God-given identity, experiencing a deep sense of belonging, and finding meaning in the world. As 1 Corinthians 12:27 (NIV) tells us, "You are the body of Christ, and each one of you is a part of it."

We believe our primary calling is to be the beloved of God in Christ. Stewarding leadership begins with discovering this identity, rather than focusing on developing particular skills. Far too often, talented leaders who are not grounded in this central identity in Christ achieve outward results but either burn out or, worse, fall into scandal. Becoming firmly grounded in this primary calling as beloved reframes every other secondary calling—in work, family, school, church, and all of life. The Table of Christ is central in this stewardship of place. As our invitation to the Lord's Table begins:

> Friends, this is the joyful feast of the people of God!
> People will come from north and south,
> and from west and east,
> and sit at table in the kingdom of God.[4]

Our primary analogy for understanding our church community is *family*. Many members of our community are Asian Americans, for whom family is a strong cultural value. We find this is a relatable way to understand our life of faith together for *all* people—and redemptive for those for whom family of origin might be a place of pain. As Jesus invites and welcomes us each to his Table, we become sisters and brothers, aunts and uncles, in Christ. Psalm 68:6 (NIV) tells us, "God sets the lonely in families." When we gather, we try to eat together as much, and as well, as

4. *Book of Common Worship*, Kindle edition, 552.

possible. As we open our mouths to the meal in front of us, we open our hearts to one another.

It is one thing to proclaim our values with words, but it is another thing to put them into practice. Innovation and risk-taking must be supported through actual systems in lived-out praxis. Stewarding Anchor City as *place* means creating a culture of acceptance and belonging, through success, failure, and everything in between.

This stewardship of *place* has been particularly meaningful as we have reached many "Dones" and their families (who, unfortunately, have often experienced wounding from past church experiences).[5] From this experience of genuine belonging, we have seen several of these families grow in leadership within the church community. For example, some have taught Sunday School or led a small group for the first time,[6] while others have even led new fundraising initiatives. This sense of *place* has created leadership outside of our church as well, through engaging in justice work, neighboring well, and becoming culture makers in their workplaces.

Stewarding Pain

Creating a place of belonging means cultivating honest conversations and self-reflection, particularly about the pain we all bear. Otherwise, leadership can create more pain and frustration. Richard Rohr notes, "If we do not transform our pain, we will always transmit it—to our partner, our spouse, our children, our friends, our coworkers, our 'enemies.'"[7]

The broader culture's answer to the problem of pain is to anesthetize ourselves to it, through self-medication, entertainment, or outright denial. This approach to pain, however, tends

5. Packard, "Meet the 'Dones.'" Sometimes referred to as "de-churched"—people who participated (sometimes quite actively) in their churches, but eventually chose to leave their church and/or "organized religion."

6. One "done" reported back to me after teaching Sunday School that she never would have thought she could teach others about Jesus.

7. Rohr, "Transforming Our Pain."

to create zombies—people who are always consuming but never satisfied. Following the way of Jesus gives us courage to live *into* our pain, and to allow him to redeem it. Dave Gibbons' insight into leadership has become an important tenet for us: Leadership, simply defined, is building trust and bearing pain.[8] If we cannot allow Christ to bear and transform our pain, our leadership will not be viable.

As a third-culture community, we understand the pain of being an outsider—whether from being thought of as "neither/nor" or from painful church experiences in the past. However, we have seen how God can redeem our pain by connecting our humanity with others, whether they are similar to us or not. Not everyone can relate to our victories or successes, but everyone understands pain and brokenness. Because all people have some form of pain in their lives, the church and its leaders are called to empathize with those who suffer while pointing toward redemption and hope. C. S. Lewis writes in *The Problem of Pain*, it is possible to "carry out God's purpose, however you act, but it makes a difference to you whether you serve like Judas or like John."[9]

Dreaming of new ways of forming Christian communities will indeed require mutuality, collaboration, and trust between established church leaders and new worshipping communities. Third-culture leadership is uniquely equipped to acknowledge the pain established leaders might feel at the loss of the past while simultaneously pointing toward a hopeful, if uncertain, future. Through their embodied witness, third-culture leaders can invite others not to be afraid of pain but, rather, to bring to it Christ's redemptive power for the world.

Stewarding Potential

I believe part of my call as a pastor is to discern and empower the God-given dreams of each member of our community. The goal is

8. Gibbons, *The Monkey and the Fish*, 144.
9. Lewis, *Problem of Pain*, 111.

not to find people to fulfill the vision of the pastors and plug them into the needs that arise from that vision but, rather, to raise up leaders who courageously join the mission of God in every sphere of their lives. As such, the shape of their potential is not limited by the scope of ministry within our local church but, rather, open-ended in kingdom possibilities.

Many people in our community bear pain around their disbelief in their own God-given ability or dreams. I have found that churched, de-churched, and unchurched people alike often believe that Christian leadership must look a certain way and they assume they do not fit the mold. I resonate with Michael Moynagh's encouragement to avoid making assumptions about leaders in new worshipping communities based on particular skills or character traits. As a pastor, I regularly pray for eyes to see the potential of *everyone* at Anchor City, particularly those who do not see themselves as, or believe they can be, leaders. One of my joys has been coming alongside people discovering their potential for leadership in all spheres of life because of their identity in Christ.

One way to steward leadership potential is through self-discovery and identity assessments such as CliftonStrengths and the Enneagram.[10] In our leadership team, and in various small group settings, we have encouraged people to take these assessments and discuss the ways the results might impact their lives. Sometimes, the results are eye opening and surprising, and they have always led to fruitful and interesting discussion. Since we value collaboration and teamwork, these assessments have also enabled deeper understanding of others as well.

We also steward potential through our theology of calling and vocation. As a church, we believe our vocation is not to create more activity within the local church building, but to send the church into all the places where God has "planted" us (work, school, home, etc.). Sometimes, when church people talk about "calling," they feel like they need perfect crystal clarity or to hear

10. You can find the CliftonStrengths online assessment at https://www.gallup.com/cliftonstrengths/en/home.aspx. The Enneagram Institute offers the Riso-Hudson Enneagram Type Indicator at https://www.enneagraminstitute.com.

the audible, indisputable voice of God in order to respond. We believe individuals are called first as God's beloved and, then, called to live this out in a wide variety of ways. These "secondary" callings are varied and diverse, meant to be lived out in the varied and diverse contexts of everyday life. In this sense, innovation and creativity are not the exclusive realm of rare inspired genius but, as Hagley observes, discerning and participating in what God is already doing, as the people God has called us to be.

Stewarding leadership potential often means pushing back against competing cultural values of comfort, wealth, or consumerism, much of which is done through weekly preaching and teaching. We recognize how difficult it can be to live out kingdom values, so we work carefully to create an environment in which, as Jesus describes in Matthew 13 (NIV), the seeds of kingdom potential are not snuffed out in their early, vulnerable stages by the thorns of "the worries of this life and the deceitfulness of wealth."

From the starting point of identifying and encouraging unlikely leaders, we seek then to develop and grow their potential by challenging them to stretch themselves. One church member, a successful consultant, demonstrates faith leadership in her workplace; not necessarily in a "traditional" sense (e.g., starting a lunchtime Bible study, etc.) but as a culture maker. As she began to see her workplace as part of God's mission, where she could demonstrate spiritual leadership through bearing others' pain, her relationships with others—particularly those with difficult personalities—became more empathetic. By embodying grace instead of judgment, she has led a shift in how her teams operate.

Another member of our community is the director of a Christian preschool. She views her work as much more than a "job," but with a deep sense of calling to her students, their parents, and her broader community. One difficult situation involved a teacher who had begun to neglect some of her teaching responsibilities. She chose to take this teacher out to lunch to find out what was happening in her life and, at the same time, to remind her of her responsibilities as a teacher. This conversation led to positive results, with her teacher rebounding and picking up her performance once again. She also sees the preschool as a mission to bring early childhood education to everyone—not just those who can easily afford it—and strives to make it accessible to all who come.

A photographer from our church community nervously taught Sunday school for the first time, learning to tie together Scripture with photography principles such as light, shadow, framing, and perspective. Beyond sharing his skills in a church setting, he has used his photography to bless and serve others throughout San Diego. Because of his empathy for families and children in need, he has set up free portrait sessions in partnership with the local Rescue Mission for mothers and children, a back-to-school event for children from an under-resourced neighborhood, and a soccer coach who works with refugee children.

One of our "Dones" has experienced a new perspective on his faith in Jesus as Anchor City continually explores the intersections of faith and justice. In our community, as he has connected his deep concern for justice with following Jesus, he has become more excited about contributing to the life of our new worshipping community. Recently, this excitement led him to lead a small group for the first time in his life. He had never pictured himself leading discussions of spiritual matters because he did not think "someone like him" should be leading, but he has found it to be a life-giving and soul-shaping experience.

The table has been a place of awakening to faith for one of our "Nones"—allowing him the opportunity to express his God-given gifts. The affirmation of his talent and love for cooking has opened up his imagination for what leadership can be. He usually shies away from official leadership positions out of humility, but demonstrates leadership, generosity, and hospitality by preparing wonderful meals. During one imaginative exercise, we were delighted to hear him respond right away to the question, "If Jesus came to your house for dinner, what would you serve him?"[11]

11. The answer, in case you're wondering, is tamales.

Stewarding Leadership

One beneficial side effect of stewarding as many leaders as possible has been the financial health of our new worshipping community. While things could always be better,[12] over the last four years we have seen consistent growth in both overall giving and an increasingly diversified mix of givers.

Certainly, church planting places many urgent demands before us. However, we resist the urge to focus on short-term results because, as Hagley observes, stewarding leaders in new Christian communities is slow relational, missional work. We recognize the long-term commitment required to cultivate leaders. One unexpected roadblock in developing leaders has been unhealthy tendencies among our churched leaders toward consumeristic views of church. We have worked to help them unlearn this "religious goods and services" mindset, pointing them toward a missional perspective. Those who are new to faith (the "Nones")[13] and those returning to faith have tended to "get it" more quickly. While we certainly commit to developing healthy faith foundations, these leaders have less church baggage and are able to respond more easily.

For us, faithfully stewarding leaders means helping *people* discover ways to live out their God-given dreams in all areas of life rather than plugging them into various *projects* within the church. When potential leaders ask us what the church needs, I often counter with the question, "What do you love?" In asking this, we have provided opportunities for leaders to experiment and grow in areas of passion and calling rather than perceived needs. In navigating and, indeed, thriving amid the uncertainty of our liminal post-Christendom future, I believe these third-culture principles will help the church steward leaders who creatively and joyfully participate in the redemptive mission of God for the world.

12. We're pretty sure we heard several "amens" there.

13. Cooperman and Smith, "Factors Driving the Growth."

Bibliography

1. Sustaining Grace

Carter, J. Kameron. *Race: A Theological Account.* New York: Oxford University Press, 2008.

Christerson, Brad, and Richard W. Flory. *The Rise of Network Christianity: How Independent Leaders Are Changing the Religious Landscape.* New York: Oxford University Press, 2017.

Cray, Graham. *Mission-Shaped Church: Church Planting and Fresh Expressions in a Changing Context.* New York: Seabury, 2009.

Finke, Roger, and Rodney Stark. *The Churching of America, 1776–1990: Winners and Losers in Our Religious Economy.* New Brunswick: Rutgers University Press, 1992.

Flett, John G. *The Witness of God: The Trinity, Missio Dei, Karl Barth, and the Nature of Christian Community.* Grand Rapids: Eerdmans, 2010.

Gay, Craig M. *The Way of the (Modern) World; or, Why It's Tempting to Live as if God Doesn't Exist.* Grand Rapids: Eerdmans, 1998.

Hanciles, Jehu. *Beyond Christendom: Globalization, African Migration, and the Transformation of the West.* Maryknoll: Orbis, 2008.

Jennings, Willie James. *The Christian Imagination: Theology and the Origins of Race.* New Haven: Yale University Press, 2010.

Jones, Robert P. *The End of White Christian America.* New York: Simon and Schuster, 2016.

Keifert, Patrick R. *We Are Here Now: A New Missional Era.* Eagle: Allelon, 2006.

Latourette, Kenneth Scott. *The Great Century.* Vol. 4, *Europe and the United States.* New York: Harper, 1941.

———. *The Great Century.* Vol. 5, *The Americas, Australasia, and Africa.* New York: Harper, 1943.

Noll, Mark A. *The Old Religion in a New World: The History of North American Christianity.* Grand Rapids: Eerdmans, 2002.

Putnam, Robert D. "Tuning In, Tuning Out: The Strange Disappearance of Social Capital in America." *Political Science and Politics* 28 (1995) 664–683.

Rotolo, Thomas, and John Wilson. "What Happened to the 'Long Civic Generation'? Explaining Cohort Differences in Volunteerism." *Social Forces* 82 (2004) 1091–121.

Smith, James K. A. *How Not to Be Secular: Reading Charles Taylor*. Grand Rapids: Eerdmans, 2014.

Sparks, Paul, et al. *The New Parish: How Neighborhood Churches Are Transforming Mission, Discipleship and Community*. Downers Grove: InterVarsity, 2014.

Taylor, Charles. *A Secular Age*. Cambridge: Belknap, 2007.

Van Gelder, Craig. "An Ecclesial Geno-Project: Unpacking the DNA of Denominations and Denominationalism." In *The Missional Church and Denominations: Helping Congregations Develop a Missional Identity*, edited by Craig Van Gelder, 12–45. Grand Rapids: Eerdmans, 2008.

———. "How Missiology Can Help Inform the Conversation about the Missional Church in Context." In *The Missional Church in Context: Helping Congregations Develop Contextual Ministry*, edited by Craig Van Gelder, 12–43. Grand Rapids: Eerdmans, 2007.

Walls, Andrew F. *The Missionary Movement in Christian History: Studies in the Transmission of Faith*. Maryknoll: Orbis, 1996.

2. A Small Shift toward Sharing All Things in Common

Board of Pensions of the Presbyterian Church (USA). *Living by the Gospel: A Guide to Structuring Ministers' Terms of Calls as Authorized by the 223rd General Assemby (2018)*. PC(USA), Philadelphia, 2019. http://www.pensions.org/file/our-role-and-purpose/the-connectional-church/living-by-the-gospel/Documents/pln-619.pdf/.

Ivanova, Irina. "Millennials Are the Biggest—but Poorest—Generation." CBS News, November 26, 2019. https://www.cbsnews.com/news/millennials-have-just-3-of-us-wealth-boomers-at-their-age-had-21/.

Jennings, Willie James. *Acts*. Belief: A Theological Commentary on the Bible. Louisville: Westminster John Knox, 2017.

Nelson, J. Herbert, II. "Stated Clerk: What Per Capita Pays for, Why It Matters." *Presbyterians Today*, January 2, 2020. https://www.presbyterianmission.org/story/pt-0120-percapita/.

Presbyterian Church (USA). *The Constitution of the Presbyterian Church (U.S.A)*. 2016 ed. Louisville: Office of the General Assembly.

———"Healthy Pastors, Healthy Congregations." http://www.pensions.org/your-path-to-wholeness/healthy-pastors-healthy-congregations.

3. Sustainability in God's Good Order

Ensign-George, Barry. *Between Congregation and Church: Denomination and Christian Life Together*. London: Bloomsbury, T. & T. Clark, 2018.

———. "Denomination as Ecclesiological Category: Sketching an Assessment." In *Denomination: Assessing an Ecclesiological Category*, edited by Paul M. Collins and Barry Ensign-George, 1–21. London: T. & T. Clark, 2011.

Heclo, Hugh. *On Thinking Institutionally*. Boulder, CO: Paradigm, 2008.

Presbyterian Church (USA). "1001 New Worshipping Communities." https://www.presbyterianmission.org/ministries/1001-2/.

4. Stewards of Grace

Caputo, John D., and Michael J. Scanlon, eds. *God, the Gift, and Postmodernism*. Bloomington: Indiana University Press, 1999.

Finke, Roger, and Rodney Stark. *The Churching of America, 1776–1990: Winners and Losers in Our Religious Economy*. New Brunswick: Rutgers University Press, 1992.

Gay, Craig M. *Cash Values: Money and the Erosion of Meaning in Today's Society*. Grand Rapids: Eerdmans, 2004.

Hall, Douglas John. *The Steward: A Biblical Symbol Come of Age*. Rev. ed. Grand Rapids: Eerdmans, 1990.

Heath, Elaine A., and Larry Duggins. *Missional, Monastic, Mainline: A Guide to Starting Missional Micro-Communities in Historically Mainline Traditions*. Eugene: Cascade, 2014.

Johnson, Kelly S. *The Fear of Beggars: Stewardship and Poverty in Christian Ethics*. Grand Rapids: Eerdmans, 2007.

Johnson, Luke Timothy. *Sharing Possessions: What Faith Demands*. Grand Rapids: Eerdmans, 2011.

Mauss, Marcel. *The Gift: The Form and Reason for Exchange in Archaic Societies*. Translated by W. D. Halls. New York: Norton, 1990.

Sandel, Michael. *What Money Can't Buy: The Moral Limits of Markets*. New York: Farrar, Strauss and Giroux, 2012.

Tanner, Kathryn. *Economy of Grace*. Minneapolis: Fortress, 2005.

Walls, Andrew F. *The Missionary Movement in Christian History: Studies in the Transmission of Faith*. Maryknoll: Orbis, 1996.

Zizioulas, Jean. *Being as Communion: Studies in Personhood and the Church*. Crestwood: St. Vladimir's Seminary Press, 1985.

5. Sustainable Churches Have Discipled Leaders

Barton, Ruth Haley. *Strengthening the Soul of Your Leadership: Seeking God in the Crucible of Ministry*. Downers Grove: InterVarsity, 2008.

Chan, Simon. *Spiritual Theology: A Systematic Study of the Christian Life.* Downers Grove: InterVarsity, 1998.
Climicus, John. *The Ladder of Divine Ascent.* Translated by Colm Luidheid. New York: Missionary Society of St. Paul, 1992.
Thrall, Bill. *The Ascent of a Leader: How Ordinary Relationships Develop Extraordinary Character and Influence.* Jackson: Perichoresis, 1999.

6. The Stewardship of Prayer and Play

Presbyterian Church (USA). *The Constitution of the Presbyterian Church (U.S.A).* Louisville: Office of the General Assembly, 2016.
Sacks, Cheryl. *The Prayer-Saturated Church: A Comprehensive Handbook for Prayer Leaders.* Colorado Springs: NavPress, 2007.
Scazzero, Peter. *The Emotionally Healthy Leader.* Grand Rapids: Zondervan, 2015.

7. Learning to Listen

Bonhoeffer, Dietrich. *Sanctorum Communio: A Theological Study of the Sociology of the Church.* Minneapolis: Fortress, 2009.
Brown, Brené. *Braving the Wilderness: The Quest for True Belonging and the Courage to Stand Alone.* 1st ed. New York: Random House, 2017.
Curtice, Kaitlin B. *Glory Happening: Finding the Divine in Everyday Places.* Brewster: Paraclete, 2017.
Garland, Diana. *Family Ministry: A Comprehensive Guide.* Downers Grove: IVP Academic, 2000.
Hagley, Scott. *Eat What Is Set before You: A Missiology of the Congregation in Context.* Skyforest: Urban Loft, 2019.
Hall, Douglas John. "On Being Stewards." *Journal for Preachers* 111 (1987) 18–23.
Smith, Christian, and Melina Lundquist Denton. *Soul Searching: The Religious and Spiritual Lives of American Teenagers.* New York: Oxford University Press, 2005.
Wiman, Christian. *My Bright Abyss: Meditation of a Modern Believer.* Reprint. New York: Farrar, Straus and Giroux, 2014.

8. Forming Generous Disciples

Bass, Dorothy, and Craig Dykstra. "A Theological Understanding of Christian Practices." In *Practicing Theology: Beliefs and Practices in Christian Life,* edited by Dorothy Bass and Miroslav Volf, 13–32. Grand Rapids: Eerdmans, 2002.

Copeland, Adam. Introduction to *Stewardship 101: An Invitation to Financial Leadership*, edited by Adam Copeland. Luther Seminary Center for Stewardship Leaders, 2017. https://faithlead.luthersem.edu/resources/stewardship-101/.

Davidson, Hillary, and Christian Smith. *The Paradox of Generosity*. Oxford: Oxford University Press, 2014.

Foster, Richard. *Freedom of Simplicity: Finding Harmony in a Complex World*. Rev. ed. New York: HarperCollins, 2010.

Kondo, Marie. *The Life-Changing Magic Tidying Up: The Japanese Art of Decluttering and Organizing*. Emeryville: Ten Speed, 2014.

Ortberg, John. "Ruthlessly Eliminate Hurry." *Christianity Today*, July 4, 2002. https://www.christianitytoday.com/pastors/2002/july-online-only/cln20704.html.

Smith, James Bryan. *The Good and Beautiful God*. Downers Grove: InterVarsity, 2009.

Swenson, Richard A. *Margin: Restoring Emotional, Physical, Financial and Time Resources to Overloaded Lives*. Colorado Springs: NavPress, 2004.

Twist, Lynne. *The Soul of Money*. New York: Norton, 2017. Kindle ed.

Westerhoff, John. *Grateful and Generous Hearts*. New York: Morehouse, 2002.

9. Democratizing Church Planting

Chen, Chao C., et al. "Does Entrepreneurial Self-Efficacy Distinguish Entrepreneurs from Managers?" *Journal of Business Venturing* 13 (1998) 295–316.

Dutton, Christine. *Mission-Shaped Church: Church Planting and Fresh Expressions of Church in a Changing Context*. London: Church House, 2004.

———. "Unpicking Knit and Natter: Researching an Emerging Christian Community." *Ecclesial Practices* 1 (2014) 31–50.

Moynagh, Michael. *Changing World, Changing Church*. London: Monarch, 2001.

———. *Church in Life: Innovation, Mission and Ecclesiology*. London: SCM, 2017.

Murray, Stuart. *Changing Mission: Learning from the Newer Churches*. London: CTBI, 2006.

———. *Church after Christendom*. Milton Keynes, UK: Paternoster, 2004.

———. *Planting Churches: A Framework for Practitioners*. Milton Keynes: Paternoster, 2008.

———. *Post-Christendom: Church and Mission in a Strange New World*. Milton Keynes: Paternoster, 2004.

Paas, Stefan. *Church Planting in the Secular West: Learning from the European Experience*. Grand Rapids: Eerdmans, 2016.

Rae, David. *Entrepreneurship: From Opportunity to Action*. Basingstoke: Palgrave, 2007.

10. Stewardship of Gifts

Barna Group. "Generations & Generosity: How Age Affects Giving." Research Releases in Faith & Christianity. September 26, 2017. https://www.barna.com/research/generations-generosity-age-affects-giving/.

Putnam, Robert D. *Bowling Alone: The Collapse and Revival of American Community*. New York: Simon & Schuster, 2000.

11. Stewardship of Leadership

Cooperman, Alan, and Gregory A. Smith. "The Factors Driving the Growth of Religious 'Nones' in the U.S." *Pew Research Center*, September 14, 2016. www.pewresearch.org/fact-tank/2016/09/14/the-factors-driving-the-growth-of-religious-nones-in-the-u-s/.

Gibbons, Dave. *The Monkey and the Fish: Liquid Leadership for a Third-Culture Church*. Grand Rapids: Zondervan, 2009.

Lewis, Clive S. *The Problem of Pain*. New York: HarperCollins, 2014.

Packard, Joshua. "Meet the 'Dones.'" *Leadership Journal*, July 6, 2015. www.christianitytoday.com/pastors/2015/summer-2015/meet-dones.html.

Presbyterian Church (USA). *Book of Common Worship: Pastoral Edition*. Louisville: Westminster John Knox, 2018.

Rohr, Richard. "Transforming Our Pain." *Center for Action and Contemplation*. June 29, 2016. https://cac.org/transforming-our-pain-2016-07-03/.